Designed and Written by Dave Conrey
www.daveconrey.com

Edited by Michele Truty
www.micheletruty.com

Author Photography by Misha Hettie
www.mishahettie.com

ISBN-13: 978-1517153809

ISBN-10: 1517153808

The Gold Is In the List

Find Your First 1,000 Subscribers Fast

by Dave Conrey

Dedicated to The Army

Table of Contents

Introduction

The Age of the Digital Sharecropper

Before we begin, I want to share a story with you about Etsy, and how that marketplace has a tremendous effect on how some sellers go about their business. Rather, how they end up out of business because of Etsy's actions. I use the handmade marketplace as a example, but this same concept could apply to eBay, Amazon, or any other online marketplace where sellers work under the oversight of a larger corporation.

If you search the Internet for the phrase, "Etsy shut down my shop," you'll get back links to the kind of stories of small-business owners having their Etsy stores shut down unceremoniously, often without any explanation. Typically this is because the person with the complaint had broken the marketplace's terms of service in regards to copyright infringement or from improper use of products or materials that were not handmade in the eyes of Etsy.

The door gets slammed in the seller's face, without access to anything within their shop. The seller, left in a lurch, wonders how to get their shop back up and running or, at the very least, reclaim any assets. One such story tells of a woman who got her shop closed because of alleged copyright infringement. Over a weekend, she had a bunch of new orders come in, but she had yet to fulfill. Then, when she logged in on Monday, her shop was closed, all access to her account details were denied, and she had no way to interact with her customers. She couldn't send out her sold orders, because Etsy completely shut her down, threatening not only her livelihood but also her reputation.

That's a huge problem, and not because she couldn't reach out to the people who purchased, but that she assumed those buyers were her customers. The reality is that while those people purchased her goods, they are technically Etsy's customers. Mind you, Etsy wouldn't be doing customer service control after the shop was shut down, and the shop owner would suffer the brunt of public disdain if her shop wasn't reopened soon. If those customers didn't get their orders soon--and they weren't getting any contact from the seller--they might take to social media to lambast her for taking their money and running out. When Etsy shuts a shop down, they don't give warnings to customers. They don't post up signs on the page saying the shop is in development. They cut the cord, and all that remains is an error page for anyone who happens to visit. The customers wouldn't have any clue that the shop had actually been shut down by Etsy, unless the seller had sent a message via social media and the customers saw it. The customers would be just as in the dark as the seller, and without any real recourse. Whatever effort the seller could make with the customers would be damage control instead of a proactive approach to keep customers in the know—the seller was on a deserted island, with no way to reach the customers until they reached out to her, if they even knew how.

This dramatized story is played out on a daily basis across the web, whether it's in marketplaces like Etsy, or social media outlets like Facebook and Twitter. Sometimes it's the fault of the business owner for not paying close enough attention to the terms of service, infringing upon someone's copyright, or being a general douchebag to others. Other times, it can arise from the malicious intent of people who want to do them harm unleashing a barrage of complaints about a shop or social media account to get them shut down. As much as we rely on these platforms to do our business and conduct our lives, we are at their mercy when we give them the control. At any moment, the platforms can use their supreme power to cut our proverbial legs out from under us--and not have to tell us a single reason why they did it.

A Brief History Lesson

Back in the years after the American Civil War, when the newly emancipated slaves could use the skills they'd honed on the plantations to build a life of their own. Because blacks were still not allowed to own land in most parts of the country, landowners would allow sharecropping on their property by giving them a chance to lease a portion of land. The landowner would charge the sharecropper a leasing fee, and come harvest time, the landowner would take a healthy portion of the harvest as payment. The landowner had all the advantages of running a farm with much less work. He had all these people to do the work for him, and he still got paid his portion of the harvest. Ironically, it was a better deal than owning slaves, because the landowner no longer had to care for the sharecropper. With slaves, the landowner had to feed, house, and clothe them. In this new deal, the sharecropping farmer paid his own way through life, and still gave a big chunk of his hard work to the landowner each season. Is this starting to sound familiar?

If a particular sharecropper wasn't making good use of his portion of land, or the harvest wasn't producing, the owner could kick the farmer off the land without recourse. All the hard work the sharecropper put into the land would be erased in a moment, and he would be forced to take what little personal belongings he and his family had and find a new plot of land to farm, starting from nothing all over again. Many times the sharecroppers were left with no way to start again, because all the seed, tools, materials, and housing had to be left on the land—a life destroyed at the whim of wealthy plantation owner. What did he care? There would be someone else willing to farm the land and pay the sharecropping fees.

It wasn't long before many of the former sharecroppers got wind that the United States government was looking to expand into the Western territories, and they hopped onto railroad outfits to forge their own path in the Oklahoma land rush. The farmers, ranchers, and craftsman made their own way, creating lives for themselves beyond the grasp of landowners. This new territory was dangerous and wild, but wide open for opportunity.

As business owners, we are sometimes enticed by property owners to use their land to turn our dream into reality. Etsy, Amazon, eBay, Facebook, Instagram, and Twitter are the owners, and we operate on their property. It all seems great because of the ease and accessibility, but it's wrought with perils we may not be considering.

When we build our house on someone else's land, we run the risk of them telling us to vacate their property, without recourse. The woman who had her Etsy shop shut down is a classic example. If only she had some way to communicate directly to her fans and customers the moment something went wrong with her shop. Although Etsy does allow you to contact customers in regards to the transaction, they do not allow you to take the customer's information for your own purposes. If those customers were told from the start to get on the maker's mailing list to get the latest updates about their purchase, the seller could have easily reached out to all of them the moment she knew her shop was down. She could have sent a formal apology for the hiccup and asked them for any logistical information so she could get the orders out on time. Instead, she relied on Etsy to be her communication tool, and it hurt her business.

Our reliance on social media is no different. If you have a Facebook page for your business, you know how difficult it is to get your message out to people, especially since Facebook adopted the "pay to play" methodology to get business owners to buy ads. Before, if you needed to communicate something in a hurry to your fans, you could post it up on Facebook, maybe multiple times in a day, and could rely that most of your fans would get the message in their news feed. Now, you're lucky if 5% or so will see the messages you post.

Sure, you can spend money with Facebook ads to get the message out, and you may want to advertise for certain messages, but if you needed to send a quick note to let people know your shop was down temporarily, you may not want to pay big money to get that information out to them. If, instead of counting on Facebook to deliver important information, you had an active mailing list for communication, that note would go out to more people, faster, and for less money.

The previous lesson goes beyond the scope of having an active email list, and touches on the concept of marketplace independence, but this book is about helping you maintain a line of communication to customers and fans. Talking about switching from Etsy or Amazon to Shopify or WooCommerce is a book for another day, but understand that it's an overlaying topic, and something to consider as you move toward self-sufficiency. For now, let's have a conversation about conversations, and learn why email is still the world's most killer app.

By the end of this book, not only will you understand the virtues of maintaining an active and engaged mailing list, but you'll learn what to share, when to share it, and how to find your writing voice. We'll discuss how to get fans on your list, where to use opt-ins, and how to entice them with value. We'll also go deep into more advanced concepts like automation, transactional emails, and managing multiple brands through email. When you close the book, you should not only feel more comfortable using email as a cornerstone in your marketing efforts, but you will have more confidence in your ability to communicate and serve customers and fans on your terms.

It is my wish that you find this information valuable enough to implement immediately into your business, which I'm sure you will, if you haven't started already. Whether you have a few dozen people on your list already, or you're just getting started, I want this guide to help you grow that number to your first one thousand subscribers, and beyond. I'm certain once you start growing your list, you will see the value of your efforts, both in the interactions you have with subscribers, but also in increased sales. Let's be honest, that's why we really want to grow a list—bigger dollar bills in our checking account. If you put the lessons in these pages into action, you will see more sales, with the added benefit of a legion of fans who will sing your praises and thank you for sharing your stories with them.

First, let's chat about the attributes of precious metals…

1

A Precious Commodity

There's an email marketing idiom that goes, "The money is in the list." I'm not particularly fond of that phrase, because it dehumanizes the people on your email list, reducing them to a dollar sign. Although it is true that the people on your email list will likely be your most devout customers, the idea of treating them as a revenue source is gross to me.

After thinking about it for awhile, I changed up the phrase to "The gold is in the list," because like gold, the people on your list are both valuable and precious. Gold is soft and malleable. If you hit it with a hammer, it bends and cracks, but if you polish it, it shines brilliantly. Same goes for your list. Treat your list as a precious commodity and it will reward you for years to come.

There are some in the business world who believe email is dead. They believe nobody reads emails anymore, because users rely on information to come to them via social media feeds. While that may be true to an extent, the truth is that email is still the last great killer app[*]. Even though email has been in existence for nearly 40 years, it hasn't needed much adaptation in that time, and still remains the main communication tool for individuals, teams, and businesses around the world.

Email has become permanently necessary. It is ubiquitous, desirable, and there hasn't been a new tool or application invented yet to take its place. Ask yourself, could you be without Twitter or Facebook for a month and still run your business? Could you do the same thing without email? Perhaps, but not nearly as easily.

---

[*] Forbes.com - "Email Is Still a Killer App, and Newsletters are Hot Again" - http://www.forbes.com/sites/kaviguppta/2014/12/15/dave-pell-of-nextdraft-email-is-still-a-killer-app-and-newsletters-are-hot-again/

The term killer app gets tossed around a lot in tech circles, but it's often misappropriated. It's important to understand the true definition of what makes a killer app, so we can compare other apps alongside email.

Miriam Webster defines killer app as[†], "A computer application of such great value or popularity that it assures the success of the technology with which it is associated; broadly : a feature or component that in itself makes something worth having or using."

Based on that definition, for something deemed as dead by some, email certainly seems quite alive. Now, you may not buy a computer just to run your email, but I bet you can't imagine going without an email app on your mobile device. If you're like most digital consumers, you check your email multiple times a day, perhaps even more than your Twitter or Facebook. I know I do, and I guarantee there are millions of others in the world who do the same. This is the basic construct of what psychologists call the Fear of Missing Out, but you may have seen it as #FOMO. You've probably suffered this when you're on Facebook, and someone posts up about how awesome the new Game of Thrones season is, but you don't have HBO. You pine for the awesomeness, and it makes you want to go sign up for the cable service just so you can talk about which popular character George R. R. Martin killed off this week.

Due in most part to the way we consume digital information, we've programmed ourselves to consistently desire to know what's going on next. This is why you see a restaurant full of people all looking at their mobile phones instead of at one another.

Now, FOMO is not a good reason to start a newsletter, contributing to the attention problem, but it is something to consider when creating a list, as well as the content you share with that list. Taking into account the attention span of readers, you can properly discern what kind of content your readers appreciate. Keep bringing the value and they will stick around. Only shell out junk...and there are other outcomes.

Because humans have this constant need to absorb information, their patience for crap is short. If they sense junk headed their way, they will bounce from you in milliseconds, and that affects how they think of you in future interactions. An individual may sign up for your email list in order to see what you're about, and they may stay on your list for awhile, but test their patience with crap content and you're dead to them. If you get people on your list but proceed to generate junk content--or do nothing but pitch them for sales--their need for newer and better information will soon learn to process anything that comes from you as worthless and forgettable. If,

† Miriam Webster definition of Killer App -
http://www.merriam-webster.com/dictionary/killer%20app

instead, you provide quality information that is valuable, interesting, and fun, then your open rates will be higher and your reader retention longer. In other words, FOMO can work for you or against you, and it comes down to the quality of the information you provide.

This brings us back to the concept of your list as a precious commodity. We are all alchemists in this digital world, but instead of trying to transmute lead into gold as some ancient alchemists struggled with, our alchemy is maintaining our precious material, not letting it devolve into something of lesser perceived value.

Break It Down

This guide is broken into three sections: theory and philosophy, strategy, and advanced concepts. In the theory section, we'll talk more about why a mailing list is a good idea for any business; why it's a living, breathing thing that you take with you wherever you go; and how it relates to the intimacy and closeness you have to your readers. I'll also discuss some cons of maintaining a list, such as the time to manage, maintain, and grow. I'll also go into the concept of the customer evangelist, why they are essential, and how to use your list to turn your readers into evangelists.

In the strategy section, we get to the nitty-gritty aspects of starting a list, email provider choices, and how to incorporate email into your marketing plan. I'll talk about what content to share, including some tips that many people are not using to their advantage. There's a bit on finding your voice, and how best to use it to speak to the people who you want to be your evangelists.

You'll learn about both the technical aspects of getting people on your list, with creative and psychological ways to entice them, doing so in an authentic and valuable way.

The advanced section is for those ready to take their list to new levels, using tools like automated response and transactional emails. That may not mean much to you now, but this will be a good knowledge base for when you're ready, and I promise to fill you in on the jargon to make it less cryptic when the need for you to grow arises. I also discuss how to manage multiple brands using one email provider, and using a list to grow sales for your products or services.

Throughout the book, there's a lot of quick, easy information to absorb and apply right away, and some stuff that requires deeper thinking. This book is not meant to be an all-inclusive guide that becomes a lifetime reference on email marketing. There's little point to having a large reference guide on this subject, because the technical information surrounding email marketing is always changing and evolving. Instead, I want this guide to be a jumping-off point for you. I want you to read the information, make quick and smart decisions about your own list, and then put those decisions into action.

The goal here is to demystify what many people feel is a complex and tricky subject to be avoided for fear or messing up. I can tell you right now, it's hard to get this wrong, but this guide is meant to help you through any tricky parts you encounter.

Finally, since we're talking about lists, you might consider joining my list, so you can see firsthand how I operate. Of course, I try hard to bring big value anytime I publish a newsletter. I want you to become an evangelist, after all. You can join the list at freshrag.com/news.

See what I did there?

The paragraph above is an example of the most direct route to getting people to join a list, but there are subtler ways. I have learned to be comfortable asking people to take action, but you may not want to, nor do you have to be as direct as me to make your list work. Everyone comes to email marketing in their own way, but we do have a goal to meet, and it's my job to make sure you get exposed to as many aspects of the job as possible.

Do You Really Need 1,000 Subscribers?

Allow me to be blunt for a moment. It is the marketer in me who wrote the subtitle, "Find Your First 1,000 Subscribers Fast." It's is a nice round number that appears large enough to warrant attention, but not so unreachable to make you feel detached from the idea. Had I said a hundred subscribers, you might not have cared, but if I said ten thousand, then you might have shied away because the number is too intangible.

The truth is, the size of your list doesn't matter nearly as much as the quality of your readers. I would much rather have a list of five hundred people who bought everything I produced, than ten thousand subscribers who were ambivalent to anything I did.

The quality of your readership should be your highest priority here. This isn't a competition to see who can amass the biggest list, but rather a pilgrimage to building a legion of readers who love you and your work, whether that's a hundred, or a hundred thousand.

Now, if you're doing amazing things and getting sales from even a modest list, then imagine what you can do with a large list. Yes, you should strive for excellence in what you put out there. Then magnify that excellence, and get more people into the fold.

2

Why You Need a Mailing List

If you've never seen anything from me before, I run a podcast called the Fresh Rag Show, where I talk with creative entrepreneurs about their business. Each month, I do a Q&A episode to give listeners a chance to ask questions of me or my guests. I love this format, because it not only solidifies my standing as some sort of authority (they're hoodwinked), but more importantly, the questions give me a gauge of what people want more information about. In fact, the idea for this book started from listening to people ask me over and over how to incorporate a list into their marketing efforts, what to write about in a newsletter, or what the purpose is of having a list in the first place.

Some believe email is an outdated way to reach out potential customers, either because they personally do not like to get spam in their email inbox, or that email isn't the cool, sexy, new social application. In terms of age, compared to the Internet, email is the responsible adult in a room of teenage hipsters. It may not be as hot as Snapchat, Instagram, or Periscope, but where it lacks in sex appeal, it gains in engagement. Email is like that rad aunt or uncle who teaches you important life lessons, has tattoos and a killer record collection, and lets you sneak a sip of beer once in a while. Like that aunt or uncle, email gets you. It will always be cool--as long as you treat it with respect.

Your List Belongs to You
We already know that the most valuable aspect of an email list is the names on that list. The more you foster a good list of email addresses, the more valuable it becomes. However, it's not the only redeeming quality. The second most valuable aspect of an email list is that it belongs to you, and

you can do just about whatever you want with it…within reason.

When you grow a group of followers on Facebook, Twitter, or LinkedIn, you're establishing credibility and connection, but those groups do not belong to you. Even if you've paid money to get more likes to your Facebook page, those fans remain the property of Facebook. Mark Zuckerberg and crew are not going away anytime soon, but if they did decide to shutter the site, you would have no way to get in touch with all the people you spent good money gathering. Suddenly, your entire fanbase becomes useless. Don't think it could happen? Just ask any rock band or celebrity that put all their energy into building up the fans on Myspace.

If instead of spending time, energy, and money building up fans on a social media site, you put that effort into building a substantial email list, your base would be nearly bulletproof. If you have a good list, and Facebook does implode, you still have a way to let people know what happened, in an instant, pointing them to the next best option of social outreach.

No matter what happens with these external sites, you remain in control of your list. Now, you will want to remain in good standing with your email service provider, because if you get all spammy on people, they will shut you down too, and blacklist you. But even they can't hold you back.

If you back up your list often, and MailChimp or Aweber shuts you down (please don't let this happen), you can still take that list to another provider. That list is yours for life, and the only way it can be taken from you is if everyone on your list unsubscribes. If that happens, well, then you've screwed up something fierce and you've got a much bigger problem to solve. Of course you know better than to let that happen, right? I'll make sure to talk about staying in good standing with the service providers later on.

Your List Is Direct

You can share all you want on your blog or in your social media accounts, but no matter how many times you post something, it still requires people to come to you. They have to come to your blog to read your posts. They must be active on their social accounts when your posts go up or they may never see them. On the other hand, send an email and your message gets delivered. Your readers don't have to show up at a certain time or be obligated to visit a special page to see your note. Your message goes to one of the few places you know they will be, and the note waits politely for them to show up. Granted, they have to actually open and read your message, and we'll talk about engagement later, but at least you know you have a better chance of getting their attention via their inbox than you ever will in a Facebook feed.

Your List Is Portable

Even if for some unforeseen reason you need to stop using the email list service you're currently on, the transition to a new one can be painless. Simply download your list in a .csv file and upload it directly to your new service provider. Where else can you build a list of engaged fans and customers and take them wherever you go, whenever you want? That function doesn't exist in any of the current social media sites—not even between sites that are part of the same organization, like Facebook and Instagram, or Twitter and Periscope. No other connective app gives you that kind of power.

Your List Is Intimate

Let's play a little memory game for a moment. Off the top of your head, answer these questions to yourself.

- Do you know anyone who uses location settings in social media even when they're at home?
- Do you know anyone who has shared pictures of their children on social media?
- Does anyone you know repeatedly share pictures of themselves in indulgent behavior (sex, drugs, alcohol)?
- How often do your closest connections share their political or religious beliefs online?
- Have you ever looked to see how many people have shared their phone numbers on Facebook?

Keeping those people in mind, what percentage openly share their email address with the public? I bet not many. In fact, you might be hard pressed to know anyone who posts their email address openly in social media. The reason is because people still regard their email address as private. They may send boob pics via Snapchat to random strangers, but they won't share their email address.

(Some might argue that a personal phone number is more private, and that would be a good debate. However, thinking of this from a marketer's point of view, accessing people via email is still regarded as standard, where sending SMS text messages to customers, even if permission was given, is considered bad form.)

I won't claim to understand the psychology of why we guard our email addresses more than anything else, but the fact is that many people use email as the last castle gate into their private world. If they give you their email address, they are inviting you to enter that private world openly.

They will be mindful and sometimes wary of your intentions, but if you start by providing quality content, then you become a trusted confidant. Maintain that relationship, and you can count on them as a valuable asset for a long time.

Your List Is Long Term

Because people don't share email addresses easily, when they do, they are expecting to hear from you on a regular basis, and for an indefinite period. Sure, some folks only want to join your list for some freebie that you may be giving away, then bail on you as soon as they get it. However, if you use the tools correctly, those types will be a small minority of your subscribers. The rest will stick with you as long as you continue to put good stuff in their inbox. Truthfully, some will even stay subscribed to you even if they may not have a need for your information anymore. I bet you are even subscribed to a few lists that you don't read much anymore. It happens to the best of newsletters. It's not great for open rate, but it happens.

The fact remains, people will stick with you as long as they feel you're bringing value and are not delivering trash to their precious space. Maintain the trust and keep your readers. I personally can't think of another circumstance where people commit to a marketing effort quite like that.

How many times have you stepped into your most favorite shop or boutique and said to yourself: "I'd really like to hear from these people on a weekly basis"? Just about never, right? I don't even want to hear from my local supermarket that often, and they're a necessity.

In the social media spectrum, with all the status updates, cute animal videos, links to listicles (articles that are nothing more than lists of things you probably don't care that much about), we do not actively seek out any particular feed from a product or service. It's rare to go a brand's website, even after a link is shared, let alone on a consistent, long-term basis. Can you think of any brand you check in with on Twitter consistently? If it's more than one or two, I'd be surprised.

Even when people visit your website, online shop, or marketplace, how often are they coming back on a regular basis because of something you did on the site? The chances are slim that this happens much, if ever. Yet, we can send out an email blast on a monthly, biweekly, or weekly basis, and people will continue to open those emails, and stick with us. That doesn't happen anywhere else in the business world.

Summing this up in a tidy way, when it comes to the value of your marketing efforts, there is none greater than your list. It's not a perfect system. Email lists do have their downsides, but pound for pound, your list will become the single best asset outside of your intellectual property. If you make great stuff, and share good things with your readers, then you have a license to mine gold...as it were.

Email vs...

Just for kicks, let's expand on the idea of how email compares to some of the other options we have as business owners. This is not meant to be a contentious debate. I'm sure that a proponent of any of the sources below would be able to bestow the virtues of each. Instead, we need to look at the weight of influence over each platform as a whole, meaning, where is your time and energy best spent?

Also, these comparisons are based on engagement and attention. There are some marketplaces in this list, but we're not talking about sales—not yet, at least. This is about eyeballs, ear drums, and click fingers.

Facebook

If you're running a Facebook business page, then you already know how atrocious your reach metrics are these days. If you're getting more than a 5% reach, you're doing something magical. The real problem with Facebook reach is that it's misleading. Just because you reached someone, it doesn't mean they paid enough attention to read what you have to say, let alone click through.

Also, when someone reads your Facebook posts, chances are you are leading them somewhere else for more information. With an email update, you can give them all the necessary information, and then if they want what you're selling, they can click.

Finally, Facebook has become a pay-to-play scenario, giving the precious attention of your followers to anyone who can outbid you. Did you know that your direct competitor can specifically target the fans of your page, and then put their branded content into your fan's news feed in front of yours--or worse, not show yours at all? Your fans don't even have to be associated with your competitor for this to happen. That's how Facebook advertising works. Contrary to that, I can promise you that once you have someone on your list, nobody will disrupt your opportunity to talk to them.

Twitter

There really is only one thing to say about Twitter in comparison to email: 140 characters. Sure, there's an immediacy to Twitter that's hard to beat anywhere else, because the timeline is always flowing and can't be disrupted just because another tweet had more retweets or was favorited more. However, it's hard to get a message out to people when you only have 140 characters to work with.

In my newsletter, I tend to write lengthy messages, sometimes a thousand words or more. Can you imagine me trying to get that information out to you via Twitter? That's an unreasonable comparison, I admit, but still valid because the immediacy of Twitter requires that I try to coax you to read a tweet first then go somewhere else to read the rest. Again, with an email, the information is already there.

Instagram

OK, pictures are nice, and having the ability to show them is great. You can show pictures in email, but Instagram really does have the whole photo thing nailed. On the other hand, once someone has looked at your photo and they move on to your text, are you going to drop all the information you have into the photo description? Can you imagine me and a one thousand-word Instagram update?

The real downfall with Instagram, at least from a marketing perspective, is that there's no way to get people over to my information cleanly. Links in the body of a photo comment are non-clickable, and they've barred you from selecting the text to copy it. If you want people to read more of your information, you either have to change your profile's link every time you want to share an update, or you give them a link in the comments they can hopefully memorize to type it into a browser. That added effort makes Instagram a marketing nightmare, at least from an action-taking standpoint. Too many steps, it requires too much thought on the part of the viewer. Make it even marginally difficult and those people will bounce.

Etsy

Yes, you can get lots of random people to your shop who may have never found you in other ways, and they may actually buy from you. However, if they do, you are only allowed to contact them in regards to that transaction. You are not allowed to follow up with them later to tell them you're having a sale, new product, or a special event. That is expressly against the Etsy terms of service.

You can't link out to your own website in any of your listings, so you can't tell people to join your email list. You can have a link to your website in your profile, but it's diminished--and if you break the rules on this, Etsy will smack you down, and perhaps close your shop without notice.

When you have someone on your email list who hasn't bought from you yet, there's still a chance they might, as long as they stay on your list. On Etsy, you don't have the slightest clue who your potential customers are. You have no way of knowing why people came to your shop and didn't buy. At least with a list, you could create a questionnaire and have people fill it out to find out why they haven't bought yet. There's no such option with Etsy, and even if you did know the information, Etsy strictly prohibits contacting potential customers that way. This all goes back to the concept that the people who by from you there are not actually your customers. They are Etsy's customers, and Etsy doesn't want you messing with their people.

Amazon

Take everything I said about Etsy, add in the aspect of not knowing a dang thing about who bought from you, and then you have Amazon.

You don't know who bought, have no idea where to contact them, and for sure can't do anything to get them back if they didn't purchase from you. In fact, it's possible Amazon sent them to one of your competitors…on purpose!

Interaction with customers and fans is limited to one area, and that's in the reviews section. You can reply to anyone who left you a review, but you cannot share any links that direct them off Amazon. That is against the terms of service, and can get you shut down.

On the upside, Amazon is a living, breathing machine, and if you play the game the right way, they will help you sell to people you would never meet (or get to talk to). Once they have your product in their hands, hopefully you've given them a way to reach out to you. For me, I ask them to join my newsletter in the first few pages of my books. That's about as much attention as I'm allowed.

Advertising

Traditional advertising is ridiculously expensive, and has almost zero effectiveness anymore. When was the last time you saw a traditional advertisement or commercial and said, "Oh man, I gotta have that widget-doohickey!" You haven't, am I right?

Some contend advertising is about branding and awareness, but there are far cheaper ways to build your brand. Even if you are advertising on a medium like Facebook, the cost of engagement will be a lot more than you will spend on an email campaign. This is especially true if you're just getting started, because you can start for free with some email service providers.

Direct Mail

OK, this one is almost ridiculous, but considering we're talking mail, I figured this might be fun. Really, though, it's almost absurd to compare the two. Do you remember when the United States Postal Service tried to get email taxed because it was cutting into their profits of putting junk mail into our mailboxes?

Direct mail is costly, non-targeted, and ineffective. Any direct mail pieces I get go from my mailbox straight into my recycle bin, aside from the occasional set of good grocery coupons, but that's only for the store I go to anyway. If the competitor sent me coupons, they would go in the trash. I'm not breaking my brand habit just because they sent me something in the mail.

Really though, who collects physical addresses anymore? I can't remember the last time I sent anything out bulk mail.

There are plenty of other comparisons to be made, but I believe this covers the spectrum. It is my opinion that none of these platforms individually work as well as email. The only way to get more attention, and better engagement, is to use two or more of these platforms together. Yet, email works pretty well all by itself.

Simple, But Not Easy

As with anything worthwhile, there are going to be both upsides and downsides, easy things, and simple things. There's a big difference between easy and simple, because easy speaks to effort, and simple speaks to concept. Email is a simple concept, but for all its awesomeness, it's never, ever easy. It would be irresponsible of me to talk about all of this without sharing the other side of the story–the part about hard work. Did I forget to mention there would be work?

If you're brand new to email marketing, then you might suffer from a bit of learning-curve-itus. Depending on which service provider you use, the technical barrier to entry will vary from slightly uncomfortable to "OMG, please make it stop!" I've been through all of these situations, and I promise to share my experience with the various services in the next section. Rest assured, there are plenty of options available that make it relatively simple to get started. When things get tough, most services have extensive support areas with a knowledge base of content to help you through the tough times. When all else fails, there's YouTube.

Once your list is up and running, the issue most run up against is scheduling. Managing a newsletter can be tedious, especially if we struggle to find content to share. More than a few times I have failed to send out an email blast because I just didn't know what to share with people. It happens to the best of email marketers, and it will happen to you. This tends to beat people down, to where they end up giving up. The best advice to getting past this is to send out something, anything, just to have it done and off your plate. Sometimes the act of writing will spur the creative juices into finding a new groove, which becomes the message.

Sticking to a schedule is also a big issue for some people. They plan on sending content out on a regular basis, but get distracted by other, seemingly more important tasks. Life gets in the way, and when we think about the sales we have to fulfill, or the more pressing business aspects to manage, sending out an email blast can take a back seat. However, I encourage you to stick to your schedule. That schedule is what your readers are counting on. If they know you're going to send out once a month, then you should make sure to put that email in their hands each month. Put it on your own calendar and commit to it. Making the commitment will help solidify your standing amongst your readers.

Some readers will hold you to an unrealistic standard. If, for instance, they got a freebie from you for getting them on the list, they may expect all the content you share to be at that level. Maybe they only want to get your free stuff, but get upset when you send out anything resembling a sales pitch. This will be a small percentage of your readers, but they will show up. They will also be the most vocal, whether that's direct to you, or spitting venom about you in their social media if you do not fulfill their specific needs.

I had one person go on a one-woman anti-Dave campaign because I refused to give her a free copy of my first book, Selling Art Online. She somehow got it in her head that I was giving away free copies, and when she didn't get one she went on a rampage, shouting it on social media, leaving harsh reviews on Amazon, and talking trash on my blog. I eventually had to put a virtual restraining order on her, banning her from my social outlets. She eventually went away to go bother someone else (which was her M.O.), but not after costing me a lot of time and energy to keep her away.

That same woman also made sure to go back and mark several previous emails of mine as spam, which is another dark side to email list building. Now, if you're generating quality content on a predetermined schedule, and your readers understand the parameters, you shouldn't have any problem. That said, being labeled as spam happens on occasion, usually because some readers do not want to unsubscribe the correct way. They can't find the "unsubscribe" button easy enough, and hit the "spam" button instead to make you go away. I would like to keep people on my list if I can, but I 'd much rather them unsubscribe then mark my notes as spam. Too many marked notes and your email service provider will lay the smack down on you. (Remember to back up your list often.)

Because most of our list-building efforts revolve around the idea of creating a legion of diehard fans who would go to the mattresses for us, all these downsides can make it tough. It may make you feel like raving fans are overrated, and you'll wonder at times if it's even worth it. You may send out message after message of good, solid content, only to be greeted by crickets when you finally ask people to buy from you.

The crickets are a fact of life at times, and should be taken with context. Hypothetically, let's assume you have a hundred people on your list right now. Given the average open-rate percentage, only about forty of those folks will read your sales message. Of those forty, only ten to twenty percent will click the links you have in your email message. If that link is to a buy page, then only a small percentage of the people who clicked through will buy. When it comes down to it, you may only get 1% of your overall list to buy from you. Most people would see that number and give up, because if only 1% buys, then what is the use of continuing?

The short answer is that it if you keep building your list, that percentage may stay the same, but the number it represents gets larger as you grow. At a certain point, the buy rate will justify the energy spent. So many sellers will spend hours on social media talking to people who have even less interest in buying from you, yet they bail on an email list at the first sign of adversity.

Like I said in the beginning, everything we do on our list is simple, but none of it is easy. The concept of email list building is basic, but the required effort is substantially bigger. Stick to it, though, and the reward can be even greater than the effort.

Do the work, make good stuff, provide value, and you will reap the rewards.

3

Putting Rubber to Road

All theory aside, now it's time to do some work. The best thing you can do for your list is something, anything, and do it today. If you have a list, great. Then ask yourself, how can you improve what you're doing? There's a lot to tackle in this section, from which provider to use to what content to share, and how to find your written voice. We'll talk about how how often to share, to get people on your list, and whether to use a freebie lead magnet to get them there. Finally, there's a section on some of the dos and don'ts I have learned from my personal list-building experience. Lots to do, so let's get started, first by answering a few rudimentary questions.

What Exactly Is an Email List Service?

This may seem almost too rudimentary for some, but I think it's good to clarify the technical aspects of email lists. At the core, your list is a database of names, email addresses, and other collected demographic information like age, sex, location (did anyone else just get a flashback to AOL?), and sometimes personal interests and preferences. It's way more complex than collecting some email addresses and sending notes to them as desired.

The information is stored on a host server (service provider), and the information is pulled together depending on the needs of the user. For instance, say you want to send a note only to you people who might be within a certain radius of you; that information can be extrapolated by simply setting a few parameters.

There's also statistical information that gets built with each interaction of your list, from the time a member of your list signs up and reads your emails, right up until they unsubscribe. All that information is collected and pieced together to provide you a better understanding of your readership. If you want to know which type of content gets read more, you can find that within the stats. Almost any questions you can think of regarding your list can be found in your stats. Granted, the longer you use your list, the more information you can extract, and it's not a great idea to focus on stats too early, or too often, because the information you get early on is skewed for lack of long-term data. Put in six to eight months of diligent effort, and then you can worry about your stats more.

How Are the Emails Created?

...and why can't I make mine pretty like that in Gmail? The truth is, you could make your emails pretty like that in just about any email program, with some extensive coding knowledge and a place on the web to store your graphics and CSS code.

The email newsletters you get are essentially web pages, coded specifically to fit into an email window. When you open up one of these emails, the email program acts like a web browser and accesses the content of the newsletter, wherever it is being hosted.

Why Can't I Use My Gmail Account?

There are many reasons why you wouldn't want to use your own email program to manage a list. First, because it would be a pain to handle. Also, you would be missing out on all the possibilities stated above, and not getting any statistics about your readership.

More importantly, if you're using Gmail, YahooMail, or a similar program as your main email provider, they absolutely do not want you to do this. It's not against their rules to bulk email, but if you do it too much, getting marked as spam more than a few times, Google, Yahoo, and the rest will blacklist you. Anything you send out, even to family and friends, will get sent directly to a spam folder.

So, yeah, don't use Gmail to send your newsletters.

What About Cost?

Some email services start as free with fees for upgrades, but most email services start between $20 and $50 a month, depending on the size of your list. There are also more advanced service providers that can cost hundreds of dollars a month, but those are more of a complete business management system, helping you operate all communication and transactions for your business. I'll go into detail about those in the Advances Practices section.

What to Look For in an Email Service

Who you choose to use will come down to finding a balance between cost and capabilities. What I recommend you do before you make a decision on a provider is to ask yourself a couple of questions:

1. What types of emails do you like and might your readers enjoy getting from you?
2. What options will you need, both immediately and into the foreseeable future?

The first question comes down to personal interests and philosophy, and should be regarded with care. If you're already providing content to fans and customers on a blog or via social media, can you identify which content people enjoy the most? Hopefully, the answer to that query is similar to what you enjoy providing.

There are no wrong answers to the first question, and you can adapt over time, so don't over think it. That said, you are going to want to tell potential subscribers what to expect from joining your list. If you tell them one thing and deliver another, you're going to get a lot of people bouncing from your list quick.

The second question is less critical, because your needs will almost certainly change, and if you've never used an email service provider, you may not know the possibilities until you're in it. However, it would be good to have at least a small idea what you want to get from the provider. Do you prefer analytics over everything else? Do you want interesting, pre-fab, graphic templates? Do you anticipate having your list grow to a certain size within a set time?

Jot down a list of all the things you feel are most essential to you, putting them in order of importance, and then measure your needs against what the different providers have available.

Lastly, look closely at some of the emails you get from other newsletters. What is it about them visually that you enjoy? What type of content do you think reads best? Also, look to see if you can find out who they are using for their service, as it might say at the bottom of the email. If not, look for a link that says "open in browser window," or something similar. When it opens in your browser, you may be able to discern who the provider is based on the URL in the browser address window.

One last piece of advice before buying into an email service is to find out how easy it is for you to export and import information from another service. There's a chance you'll be moving from one service to another over time because the one you're in doesn't quite fit your needs. Moving your list is relatively simple, but some providers require double opt-in as a security check. What this means is if you upload a list to their service, they will automatically send a notice to all the subscribers on the list telling them they need to opt in to your newsletter again. The problem here is that many people will either choose to not opt in again, or they may not see that email come through and not get the chance to reply.

Your subscriber number will take a hit, and maybe that's OK, because some of those subscribers were just waiting for the right reason to unsubscribe anyway. If they want off your list, they weren't your ideal reader, and you're both better off parting ways. The people who don't get the message, though, that's a problem because until they opt-in, the service provider will not let you send them any messages, even to remind them to opt in again. Those few people who may want to be on your list but don't know they need to take action will be lost to the wind.

One of the reasons I like Mailchimp is because they do not require this double opt-in for imported email addresses, only new ones who join through a sign-up form. It was a much smoother transition going from Aweber to Mailchimp than the other way around, let me tell you... Which I will, in the next section.

[NOTE: After I wrote this book, I was alerted by a reader that Aweber recently changed their stance on this double opt-in requirement for importing lists. Perhaps my leaving helped make a much needed change happen at Aweber headquarters. At least that's what I'm going to believe.]

The Elusive Best Provider

Let's get this out in the open right now: There is no one right choice. When it comes down to picking who you want as your email service provider, you have myriad choices, and each one has both pluses and minuses. I couldn't possibly try them all without going broke in the process. Even if I did, there's a high chance all my research would be out of date by the time I finished. It's like those guys who paint the Golden Gate Bridge—taking them several years to finish, and by the time they're done, they have to start from the beginning again. Or so the urban legend goes.

For the purposes of this section, I will talk a bit about the three services I have personally tried: IContact, Aweber, and Mailchimp. To make your decision a bit more complicated, I went ahead and added a list of all the service providers I could find in the Resources section in the end of the book—no details, just names and links. I'll leave the heavy research up to you, but if you want a no-nonsense decision made for you, go with Mailchimp. You'll find out why in a moment.

IContact

It's been several years since I first tried IContact, and I can assume that their site and service has changed quite a bit in that time. I hope so, for their sake, because my experience was less than great. The reason I chose them back then was because when I was weighing my options, their name kept coming up in comparison with Aweber and Constant Contact. The latter two were the providers of record back in the initial days of automated email marketing, but they both seemed complicated and expensive for something I was unsure I wanted or needed at the time.

IContact had many of the same benefits as Aweber and Constant Contact, but it was far less expensive than the others. I was also looking at the fledgling Mailchimp back then, because they had a free option, but when I dug into Mailchimp's early services, they lacked a lot of the fancy bells and whistles I thought I needed; bells and whistles that IContact had, for a marginal fee.

It didn't take me long to figure out that IContact had some major technical issues. My emails blasts were constantly being abandoned by the service, and they had this automated spam checker that kept me from sending my notes because it thought my headlines were too spammy in nature. I also had some big issues with tech support and customer service.

After my final run-in with tech support, I gathered my tiny list and took it over to Mailchimp. I still wasn't ready to make the leap to Aweber yet, so I stuck with Mailchimp for about a year, not being very active on it.

At the time, I think IContact was suffering from severe growing pains, and not fairing well. I'm assuming they have since improved all those aspects, because they are still around, but after too many bumps on the head, I decided to leave them behind. They may be a viable option now, so I encourage you to look at their offerings, check some more current reviews, and then do your own decision making.

Aweber

In 2013, when I was forced to take my business seriously (I got laid off at my day job), I decided to focus more on building my list. While I was still using Mailchimp, I was looking for something else again, for one very distinct reason: Mailchimp did not want people using affiliate links in their emails, for whatever reason. The act could get you shut down by the monkey, and I didn't want that, especially since I was running a several affiliate deals at the time.

I looked to Aweber this time, because they were open to affiliate marketing, and they had a stout affiliate program themselves. If I was going to be actively using and paying for a service, I might as well see if I could get paid for referring it. I did in fact get paid quite well for a short while at Aweber, but then something went critically wrong with my account.

As much as Aweber was touted by customers for their excellence customer service, I can't say that I experienced it. At some point during my stay with Aweber, people stopped getting my emails. I got message after message from readers telling me that they hadn't seen anything from me in months. When I brought this up to Aweber, they tried to tell me it wasn't their fault. They said the messages were going out and that it was probably an isolated incident with individual readers. After hearing this same canned message for the third time from a different tech support employee, I decided to pack my bags.

At the time this mess with Aweber was going down, I heard rumors that Mailchimp had overhauled their service and their interface. They also had done away with the anti-affiliate policy, and that solidified the decision for me to jump back to Mailchimp in 2014, where I've been ever since.

Something else about Aweber is that they were technically way behind the times. They had not incorporated any sort of mobile app for their service, which isn't a deal breaker but was definitely a check against them. They've since added an app, but at the time of this writing, it provides status and statistics, but you cannot construct or send campaigns. I blame that on their out-of-date email builder technology. With the rest of the world moving to responsive design, Aweber is still stuck in the HTML 4.1 world. They either do not want to adapt or can't grow fast enough, which is unsettling for such a well established tech company.

Plenty of people use Aweber still, but I will never go back to them, even with a major overhaul of their services. They've proven that keeping up with technology isn't a priority, and now that I've seen what a good email service can be, I can't imagine ever trusting Aweber again. I just don't see them surpassing Mailchimp in usability.

Mailchimp

Want to know the main reason I will stick with Mailchimp as my provider from now until the day they shut the doors (or do site wide changes that messes with my ability to do work)? When I grabbed my list from Aweber and brought it back to Mailchimp, they did not require me to use a double opt-in. Everyone who was on my list on Aweber got on my list at Mailchimp. That was win #1

Win #2 for them is simply their design aesthetic. Being a graphic artist by trade, having a unique, modern interface that was easy to use was an important factor for me. Mailchimp is all those things. On top of that, their first pay level for the service is zero! You don't have to pay to use the service as long as you have fewer than two thousand subscribers across all lists, or you send fewer than twelve thousand messages a month.

The downside to the free account on Mailchimp is that you don't get access to some key features, like statistics and campaign automation. I can no longer operate my list without automation, because I need the ability to send a series of messages to people, delivered based on when a person signed up for my list. This may not be a priority for some, but once you get a taste for it, it's hard to go back.

Even though I started on the free account, I knew right away that I was going to need to upgrade soon. The cost of the upgrade was minimal, though, and with it, I got instant access to a bunch of new tools to help me stay engaged with my readers.

Between the added functionality and the best tech support resource I've seen from any company, let alone email service providers, I do not anticipate leaving the Mailchimp anytime soon.

Full Disclosure: From this point forward, for the purposes of consistency, if I give an example of a function or tool I'm using, assume I'm talking about using Mailchimp. If there's ever ambiguity, or I switch topics, I will make sure to call out the change.

I'm a full-blown evangelist, and I share the company here strictly as a devout customer. Although I do have an affiliate account with Mailchimp, they are not paying me anything to write this book.

Mailchimp is free to start, easy to use, beautifully designed, and has a thorough knowledge base. What's not to love? In fact, you might as well go ahead and sign up for a free account on Mailchimp right now (mailchimp.com), if you haven't already. That way you can follow along without any hitches.

Starting From Scratch

In this section, I'm going to share a play-by-play of getting started with an email service provider, laying down the basic functionality, defining nomenclature, pointing out potential stumbling blocks, and addressing the need for upgraded features. Again, I'm using Mailchimp for this example, but many of the aspects here will be mimicked in almost all email service providers. If you already have a service provider and know your way around the interface well, then you may want to skip this section. Otherwise, let's boogie.

Prepping for Early Success
Before you start an account with your provider, it's a good idea to consider a two things first:

1. What is the core content you want to provide?
2. How do you want to attract people to sign up for your list?

Don't feel like you need these answers right now. I'll discuss both in detail, so you when you do start your account, you can jump in with confidence.

Understanding what you want to share will help determine the visual aspects of your chosen delivery method. Knowing how you want to get people on your list allows you a chance to set up any bonuses you provide early on. You don't need a freebie or giveaway to start a list, but if you have an idea for something, it helps engineer the process of getting that information in their hands. None of this is imperative to getting started, but it helps. I started my list without any of this information, and I tweaked as I went. It does take more noodling after you launch without these questions answered, but that should not stop you from moving forward.

Mailchimp Jump Start
Instead of a full-blown tutorial, I'm making this more of a user experience tip guide. There are plenty of solid tutorials within Mailchimp to help you through the process, but they don't always talk about best practices for smooth starts. For instance, when you are getting started, choosing an account name and which email address to use is important. I like to keep this information as general as possible, not specific to any one brand or product I might be managing. The point being that I can manage all that information within the separate lists that I start within my account.

By keeping my login information more general, or directed to my personal email, I cut down on the chance of 1) having login issues if I ever lose or cancel a web domain, and 2) it's easier to remember, because I don't need to recall which brand name I used as my login.

That's your first nugget of gold you won't find in the Mailchimp knowledge base. Stick it in your pocket while I help you find some more.

The Feds Are Watching
I don't recall the exact year, but awhile back, the Federal Communications

Commission put forth some strict standards for bulk emailing, in an effort to curb rampant spam and potentially hazardous messages that proliferated viruses. To comply with FCC regulations, all service providers require you to enter your contact information and physical mailing address, which appears at the bottom of any email message sent from a provider. Sorry, it's the law, but you have option. You do not have to use your home address if you would rather not. In fact, I recommend getting an inexpensive post office box, even if you don't use it for any other reason. It's a tax write-off, anyway.

You could also choose a fake address instead of using a PO Box, but I do not recommend this. If the service provider finds out it's fake, or the feds see it for some reason, you could get shut down and be subject to massive fines. Don't tempt fate.

Of course, you could use your regular home address if you want. We already talked about the lack of privacy we're comfortable with as a society, and while you're ramping up your list, you might be OK with having a few people know your home address. But over time, you might consider upgrading to a PO Box—because stalkers.

Terminology Confusion

One thing that you will find, if you ever switch from one email service to another, is that they use different terminology to describe similar things. There isn't a universal jargon for much of this stuff, unfortunately, but this short guide will give you insight to MailChimp's key terms, especially the ones I personally found most unclear at the start.

If you're looking at the MailChimp interface while you're reading this (because why wouldn't you), you'll see that I'm following the content of the page in order. Follow along, won't you?

Dashboard

Where you start each login, and where your core information is presented, including list growth, open rates, click-through rates, new subscribers, and ugh, unsubscribes (marked in red, as if you needed special attention to them).

Campaign

This one confused me the most at the start, because when I think of a campaign, I think of a collection of assets brought together to share a universal idea or plan—think advertising, marketing, or PR campaign. MailChimp's definition is more singular. The simplest way to look at a campaign is as a single email blast you want to send to a either a portion, or the entirety of your list. Each email you send is a campaign. I think it's a terrible term, the way they use it, but a minor obstacle overall.

Campaign Folders
Use these to organize and group campaigns together to make them easy to find—a campaign of campaigns, if you will.

Templates
A collection of predesigned layouts for your email blasts. You can choose based on the various page sections, columns, themes, and purpose. You can also adapt and save new templates once you establish a look you're comfortable with. This helps when building new campaigns, because you don't have to rebuild each new email from scratch.

List
Pretty straightforward, this is a collection of names, email addresses, and other information you can use to send specialized content for a given company, brand, or purpose.

Reports
Yeah, so, this is where the reports are. Most of this is off limits unless you upgrade to a paid account, but you can get some stats on campaigns.

Automation
One of the most powerful tools MailChimp provides...to paid users. Free account holders do not have access, but once you read more about the capabilities, it might turn you into a paid subscriber anyway. The quick and dirty explanation is that automation is a way to manage a series of email blasts that go out to people based on a set of dates or actions. You may have also heard this referred to as a drip campaign.

If you wanted to give someone a freebie tutorial about how you do something, but you wanted to give it to them over a series of separate emails while also giving them reasons to buy something from you with each email, then you would do this with automation. That's just scraping the surface of what is possible. I might just blow your mind later on.

Segmentation
This was my second biggest head-scratcher when I first started because

when you first dig into them, they sound like the same thing. Segments and groups are both tools to help organize people into categories you can later use for sending specialized messages. The key difference is that segments are for your internal use, and groups are for the subscribers.

For segments, let's say you wanted to partition your list into people who were local, and those out of the area, you can do that with segments. This would be helpful if you wanted to send a note about an event you were hosting and you didn't want to bother the people outside of your area. Depending on what kind of information you collected from your subscribers upon signup, you could segment based on many different parameters. There's a whole bunch of play to be done here, but it's more of an advanced technique. Plus, this works better once you have more members on your list.

Groups work a bit different because this is you allowing your subscribers to pick what kind of content they want to receive. If you sell products, but also like to teach about how you make the things you sell, you may want to establish groups for each type of content. This way someone who just wants to buy your stuff, but has no interest in how you make it, can choose to be part of one group instead of the other. They could also be part of both, which almost makes groups moot, but whatever.

The point is that you are giving them an opportunity to decide what they get in their inbox. The upside to this is that you get higher open rates on your emails because the information is specialized to the subscribers' interests. On the other hand, it means you're managing more types of content. (Cue the sad trombone.)

Side Note: When I use the term segmentation throughout the book, I'm referring to the general idea of portioning people into different parts of your list. I consider both segments and groups as types of segmentation. I want to make that known now to avoid confusion when it comes up again.

Merge Tags

This is a way to integrate certain information into an email blast when it goes out. Have you ever gotten an email that had your name in the headline or in the body? Most likely that was done with a merge tag.

You can use merge tags in your emails, but of course, you need to collect that information. If you're only collecting email addresses, then the merge tag for names will not work. If you want to guarantee you have the information, make sure to make the name fields required when someone fills out your sign-up form.

There are a bunch of other terms I could go into, but these are the ones you will come across most often. MailChimp has their own glossary that you can look up on their website, so if you're a term nerd, go nuts in that section of the knowledge base. This short list should be more than enough to get you started.

Notifications
(or what you don't know won't hurt you)

When you first get started creating a list, you'll be asked some questions regarding the list details. All of the questions are straightforward, but I want to give one small warning about an option you have at the bottom of the list creation page.

You'll be given a choice to get notifications about who subscribes and unsubscribes, either in a daily email, or as each person comes and goes. It is my opinion that you should not check ANY of these boxes. Yes, it can be great to get messages each time you get a new subscriber, because it validates your need for the list, but these notifications come with a price.

First, if you get a note each time someone subscribes and you end up getting a flood of new subscribers, your own inbox is going to overflow. This is more of an annoyance than anything else, but will grow tiresome, even if you're only opening a few a day.

Getting a single daily message about all the new subscribes and unsubscribes is more tolerable, but it comes with teeth. I don't care if you signed up a hundred new people in a day, if you get just one unsubscribe that day, it will hurt, maybe only a little, but some. No matter how pragmatic you are about knowing that not everyone is going to want to stay on your list, it still sucks to get notes in your inbox telling you how many people bailed on you that day. There's absolutely nothing of value in getting these emails.

Some might argue that this helps you identify who is leaving, and why they are leaving. I understand that point of view, but the reasons people leave can be wildly varied. Even if they left because they get way too many emails, our brains are genius about concocting a story about what that really means. You might believe they think you suck, which is rarely true, but that's what we like to believe when someone leaves us.

These aren't your people. They may like you, appreciate your work, but they aren't the ones who will sing your praises, or buy your stuff. If they leave, then they are doing you a favor and clearing the way for people who are of that ilk. So, let them go, and bid them farewell with kindness. You've got bigger things to worry about.

Now, for those people who think checking that last notification box that sends you a note each time someone unsubscribes is a good idea, you're just a glutton for punishment. I can't think of a more masochistic action. If that's your kind of kink though, get down with your bad self.

Sign Your Life Away

The most effective way to get someone on your list is to allow them to sign up via a form on your website, social media, or third-party application. Mailchimp gives you the capability of creative basic forms right from the dashboard. They aren't necessarily the prettiest, but they get the job done. If you have coding knowledge, you can alter the code to make them a little sexier, but the simple ones should be enough for most individuals.

To get a form started, go to the Lists section, and click on the list that needs a form. On the next page, click the sign-up forms link and that will take you to a page with a few different options: general forms, embedded forms, subscriber pop-up, and form integrations. You also get forms for your Facebook business page, and as a tablet app, if you are at an event and you want to add people to your list on the fly. Most of the time, you'll be using either a general form or an embedded form.

General Forms

These are sign-ups you create that live on Mailchimp's server. When you create them, you use a link to send people to that page to sign up. This is good if you want to use a clickable graphic that sends people to a form, or if you want to give people a quick link to jump to for sign-ups. Let's say you bought a domain name that was JoinMyAwesomeList.com. You could point that domain straight to a general form and get tons of followers quick and easy. Granted, you may get a lot of random people joining without knowing why. So, yeah, tread with caution there.

If you use a third-party application to get sign-ups, they will most likely ask you to create a basic form, and then the app will use the link you provide as the base for their integration. If you're familiar with LeadPages.net, the list-building service that provides prefab templates for sign-up forms, webinar opt-ins, and sales pages, this is the function they use to move people to your list.

Before you go any further, make sure you create at least one sign-up form and grab the link so you can share it with your fans and customers right now. Post it on your social media, and start getting people on the list today. You can give them some basics about what you have planned to offer them for being on the list, but for now, just go ahead and get some warm bodies in there.

Embedded Forms

These are similar to general forms, except you have a little more control over the design of the page. This is good because once you create a form, you're given a snippet of code to use on your site. This will embed the code right onto the page, which means your new subscriber never has to leave your site just to sign up—win/win.

Again, these embedded forms have a rudimentary design, and the code may produce a look that is a little incongruent with your site design. To fix this you can muck with the CSS code yourself, or you can hire a coder to help. If all this code talk makes you itchy, like it does me, Mailchimp has a stable of code professionals who you can reach out to for help. You can find them at http://experts.mailchimp.com.

Subscriber Pop-Ups

These are exactly what you think they are: a box that pops up on the page after a certain amount of time, obstructing your view temporarily so that you have a chance to join that site's list. The use of pop-ups are hotly debated because they are, at worst, obtrusive, and at best, the most effective way to get someone to sign up to your list. I use them, have never had anyone complain, and when I incorporated them into my site, it drove sign-ups through the roof. People say they hate them, but they work. My best advice is to experiment with pop-ups, but make sure they are easily removed. Nobody loves a pop-up that's impossible to get rid of, and I don't understand why some sites still use that sleazy technique.

Creating a List

Of all the things you'll do in your email program, this is one of the simplest. With Mailchimp, the process is easy, and can be done within a few clicks. Go to the Lists tab in the navigation, and then hit the button that says Create a List. Click it and you're on your way.

Fill out some basic details, and BOOM, you have a list. It's empty, but it's ready for you to get started. I recommend you add yourself as a contact on the list so that you get sent all the emails you end up sending to others. It's a good quality control practice to read through emails multiple times before you send them, making sure to eliminate any problems like typos, but I also recommend reading the note again after it goes out. There's something to seeing the note in the context that others do that helps understand how to make your messages better.

That's pretty much all there is to creating a list, and now you just have to get more names on it. You can do that a number of ways, such as sign-up forms on your site, importing another list via a .csv file, or adding them one at a time manually. There are also some third-party apps, like Selz.com, that will capture email addresses from every sale you make, importing the information into your list, with the customers permission, of course.

Selz is a service that helps people sell goods and services using credit and debit cards without the need to invest in a merchant account. There are others out there, like Gumroad and Square, but not all services give you the ability to import directly to a list, segment, or group like Selz.

When creating your first list, you'll be asked if you want to create groups for the list. If you feel like your readers want to partition themselves based on the information you're sharing, then you'll want to set up groups now. I talk about segmentation of your list in detail later, but just know that it's a good way for you to organize your readers for more personalized engagement.

One of the debates I used to have with myself often was when I came out with a new product, service, or brand; I struggled with understanding if I should set up a new list, or just partition people into a group. The way someone finally explained it to me is if you are creating special sign-up forms or opt-in freebies within the same brand, then you want a segment or group. However, if you have completely separate brands (Fresh Rag vs. Dave Conrey, the creator of things), then you'll want different lists for both. This also is the case if you have stand-alone products that might have the appearance of being underneath a particular brand.

I originally started my Creative Badass Challenge as a function of Fresh Rag, but when it became a much larger project in development, I knew it needed to stand on its own, so I have it on a separate list. This has both positive and negative aspects, because although I can talk independently to those two groups, and people on the two lists are there for totally different reasons, I still end up with a reasonable amount of duplicate email addresses. Also, if I ever did want to speak to both lists, I would need to send separate emails out to each list. This is a bit of a pain, but a manageable one. There are more advanced service providers that make this possible through some heavy integration, but it's way more than I currently need. I do talk about these providers in the Advanced Practices section so you have a basic understanding of their capability.

Speaking to the People

Now that you've gotten through all the basics, it's time to reach out to your people and send your first campaign. Granted, you need people to actually be on the list, so hopefully you've already created a general form and started sending people to it. If not, go ahead and do that now—no point in sending an email campaign to nobody, right? Let's populate that list.

Once you do have some people on the list, then you get to talk to them. There's a number of ways to go from here, but I recommend your first note be a detailed message about why you are sending them emails. You should remind them why they are on the list, and then tell them all that you have planned.

This post should be about information only, putting their mind at ease that you won't be sending them sales messages at every turn. Remember, the gold is in the value you provide them, and it's best to start on the right footing.

From the Campaigns page, click the create campaign button, and you'll be given choices as to what kind of campaign you want to send:

- Regular: Standard HTML-based email
- Plain Text: Text only with no dynamic content. Links are shown adjacent to the body copy
- A/B Split: For testing how different headlines or content work. Best for promotional content
- RSS-Driven: Allows people to subscribe to your blog feed via email

Most of your messages will fall within either regular campaigns or plain text, but really, regular. Plain-text emails are strictly for sending notes to a segment of people you know who do not allow graphical emails in their inbox. This is a small percentage of the population, and you can provide your readers the option of viewing each message as plain text, so it's almost redundant. If you feel like you have a need for that, go for it, but remember that it will be less pretty and more about the function and content. That might not be so bad after all.

Once you've selected your type, you'll choose which list to send it to, if you have more than one. And then you can choose whether to send to the entire list, a segment, or a particular group. This first email should go out to everyone, so choose that one this time around.

Setup

On the Setup page, you'll add a campaign title, and an email subject. The title is for your reference only, and the subject is what your readers will see. The subject line is important to consider, and it's a honed skill. This is why some people use A/B split campaigns—to test different subjects to see which ones hit best with their subscribers. In the Resources section, I've included a link to some helpful subject line writing tips. Ultimately, it comes down to knowing what makes your readers tick, and you may not know that until later down the road. Personally, I like to go for the funny or the shocking, but you may like a more direct or subtle approach.

The Setup pages has plenty of options for you to pick, but for now, let's just move through to the next section. If you want to get more acquainted with the different options, have fun, but most of them will relate better once you have more time in the proverbial command chair.

Templates

The Template page is where we get to have a little fun, but may be a bit overwhelming at first. Having a lot of options to choose from is awesome, but too much choice can cause you to get stuck, and lose momentum. My recommendation is to pick something that has the kind of layout you appreciate, and keep the design elements simple.

You can start with a blank slate template; a predefined but empty layout with a varying columns and features, or a pre-designed template with placeholder images, ready for you to punch in your text where it's marked on the template.

Whatever you choose, once you have defined a design style you appreciate, you can save your design as a new template. That way you can always go back to that design whenever you send a note for that particular list, segment, or group.

For the purposes of this first message, we should keep it simple, a single-column design, maybe with a logo at the top of the page. In the Design section, you can add images easily, change out any default placement text, and tweak the template to your heart's desire. Nothing is set in stone, so pick one and push on to the next tab.

Design

When it comes to the design elements of the page, Mailchimp has an extensive set of tutorials on how to manage this part of the message, and they can explain it far better than me, with visuals. Go to the Help section and type in "Create a Campaign with Campaign Builder," and that will take you directly to the best dang tutorial to help you through this section.

The few tips I can add to the mix is to play around with the CSS settings of the template. When you're in the design section, focus on the right panel, specifically the tabs labeled Content, Design, and Comments. Click the Design tab on the right panel, and below that will show you several more choices, like Page, Preheader, Header, Body, Footer, Mobile Styles, and Monkey Rewards. Within the first four choices, you can adjust the typography and colors of the various sections of the page.

If you're playing in this area, remember to be thorough with your changes, and try to keep to a simple palette for typefaces and colors. If you have branding colors, you can switch to them here. Your typeface choices are extremely limited, so don't get too down on yourself if you can't find a particular Google font—it won't be there. Pick the next best typestyle instead.

Mobile styles are all about making things look pretty for people who view your campaign on a mobile device. Considering how more and more people are viewing their content on mobile devices, it's a good idea to keep this simple, and aligned with your branding. If you have something that looks good to you, and you feel you might use this design again in the future, save it as a template in the options at the top right. It's easy, and it will stick with you for as long as you maintain your account.

Monkey Rewards is simply Mailchimp's affiliate program. If you activate this section, you could potentially get rewarded if anyone signs up for a paid account through your link. Speaking of links, here's mine: http://eepurl.com/ZZber. (I wouldn't be myself if I didn't at least do that much.)

Confirmation

The Confirmation page is your fail-safe. This is where you dot your Ts, cross your Is, and commit to being OK with whatever happens next (and yes, Rebekah, I mixed them up on purpose).

You'll have a laundry list of things to check through to make sure everything is copacetic. Just make sure you don't have any red flags, and you should be good to go.

If all things are good to go, then you can either hit send or schedule. Send will do just that, send it right away to all recipients. Schedule, on the other hand, will allow you to pick a date and time to send the message out. This is a good idea if you find yourself awake in the middle of the night, writing a post you just had to get out of you, but have no intention of sending it until morning.

Mailchimp even incorporates some smart sending options, like sending the blast in staggered bursts, to see if you get a higher open rate. You can also send with Timewarp, and deliver it to your recipient based on their time zone. If you felt like your message needed to be in everyone's email inbox by noon their time, then you would set up Timewarp to do just that. I've tried this technique and am not certain on its effectiveness, but I'm guessing it has something to do with delayed release of other products or content.

The final setting is something I use often, and that is to let Mailchimp decide what is the best time to send the message. They know through their analytics what is the prime time of day for your readership, during that particular day of the week, and prescribe when to send the message. Mailchimp is smarter than me, so I take whatever it says, and I execute on that wisdom. To send a note this way, you must have at least five hours left in the day that you are planning on sending the note, otherwise it will tell you to try again.

Now all you have left is to hit that dreaded send (or schedule) button. If you're like me, this will be one of the scariest moments in your business life, because, "Now they're going to see how dumb I am!"

Relax, you'll be fine, the readers will be fine, and the world will survive another day. Now breathe, and click away.

What Makes a Good Newsletter

With the basic technical details behind us, it's time to move onto making the best newsletter we can come up with for the sake of the readers. That is why you started your business in the first place, right—to provide high-quality content to make people love you and want to share your work with their friends? Good, then let's make some art.

Whenever I advise someone to start an email newsletter, their next question is almost always, "But what do I write about?" Not only is this question impossible for me to answer, because what you write about needs to come from within you, but the question is also a little bit uncreative, because you can write about whatever you want. There are almost no rules as to what you can write about, and unless you go off trying to be Spammy Spammerton, anything you put into your newsletter is fair game.

Now, if what you are really saying is, "I don't know what to share," then the focus changes, and it goes back to what I said earlier about identifying what you believe your fans and customers want to get from you. The first thing to get clear about is that you don't need to share a lot. The amount of content is less important than how you connect with your people on a level beyond "Hey, buy my stuff."

I write long-form content for my newsletters because I dig it. My updates almost always revolve around the subject of success for creative business owners (big surprise), but I deviate every now and then, just to shake things up. I've written about the birth of my son, the emotions around getting laid off, and how my first European vacation affected me as a creative. I write about health and fitness, pop culture, music, or anything else that rolls around in my head, but I always tie it back to the main theme of helping creatives with their work. These subjects work for me, but you have to decide for yourself what will serve your readers best.

It's also important to understand whom you are writing to, and what their motivation is for signing up for your list. Are they hoping for insights on how you do the work you do, or do they want to know when you post new stuff? Do they want a backstage pass to how you operate your daily life, or do they want your opinions on the industry?

Your top priority is fulfilling the promise you gave the readers when they signed up. If you told them you would send updates of new products, sending out a post that talks about your daily life might not be what they want to read about. Consider your people, then define the parameters about what topics you cover. If they know going in that it might be a mix of things, then you won't have a problem.

If you know who you want to talk to, and how often you want to post, figuring out what to share becomes simple. First rule: It shouldn't be a pitch fest! Some retail brands can get away with sending out messages that only sell, but chances are, those brands are offering up some form of compensation for the readers' time, most commonly a coupon code or a special subscriber-only sale. Those are great ideas, and you might consider them, but also think about how you can enrich the lives of the readers. Can you give something away that's free, whether that be knowledge or even an product?

Another popular technique for the artistically inclined is to give away monthly desktop wallpapers, or design templates, if that's what your reader likes. A jewelry designer may give away a guide on how to accessorize an outfit with their latest pieces, or maybe it's tips on how to pick the right piece for a loved one. A graphic artist could give away design tips on video, and a fashion designer can share a style guide for each season. Think about your products, and figure out what your reader would love to get, and then give it away freely.

I once saw a small-business owner provide a report in her newsletter of all the major recent happenings in her industry, namely the cost of doing business. She didn't come right out and say she was raising her prices, but if I had to guess, it seemed like she was prepping customers for a price increase. I'm not sure if she planned on giving that kind of report again this year, but if she created a more in-depth annual report, it could become a resource that people in her industry find useful and turn to in anticipation each year. Valuable information like that gets shared often, making her an authority people trust.

Dig deeper and provide value. Value is relative to your readers, but here are a few ideas to get you started:

- Post up progress photos and final shots of new work available in your shop.
- Let subscribers know if you're attending events locally, or out of town. Perhaps give a special code for a discount for event attendees.
- Share updates on experiments you're playing with in your work. Post some photos, and ask people what they think.
- Ask your subscribers if they have any questions about the work

you do. The next update(s) should be the answers to those questions.

- Talk about changes in the industry, either from a business owner or a consumer standpoint. Express an opinion, and people will resonate with you. Take the opportunity to ask people for their thoughts. Start a conversation.
- Write about your personal experience selling, maybe tips about what you've found successful.
- Showcase the work of people you admire. Do a top ten post of your favorite businesses. Go deeper and pick out separate niches to focus on, and you could have content for several updates.
- Take that idea above and do a list post on just about anything that relates to your business (tools, online resources).
- Give a shop tour by sharing all the tools and products you use to do the work you do.
- Start a tutorial series in which you show your process for a large project, or even small tips you've discovered that helped with productivity.
- Share your reading list. (Hint: this book should be on it.)
- Do a one-on-one interview with a fellow business person.
- Share the story of a featured customer or subscriber.
- Send a post offering big discounts on items you're trying to close out.
- Ask people to share pics of the things they've bought, and then give a coupon to them and a friend.
- Send out a list of recent posts from other blogs that you've read and found insightful or inspiring.
- Write about your history as a creative, and how you got started.
- Write about the history of the type of work you do.
- Hold a contest where people can win something from your shop. Encourage sharing.
- Once or twice a year, say thank you to all your fans.
- Do an end-of-year/-month wrap-up and talk about the future.

The limits are only as far as your own imagination. If you're ever stuck for ideas, look to websites and blogs that you enjoy, and dig through their content for inspiration. Avoid outright copying what they've done, but use the posts as a template for your own rich content, creating posts specifically for your people. As long as you stay on message, and maintain trust and consistency, you can post almost anything and people will eat it up.

Finding Your Voice

One thing many people struggle with, especially those new to writing and sharing their thoughts, opinions, and wisdom, is how to express themselves properly. In writing circles, this is described as finding your voice, and it means the unique way you express yourself. When first getting started, you may not know anything about your voice, let alone how to share it. Most people in this situation will start out by doing what other people do, sharing what other people share, and posting the types of content they see others posting. Although common--and an effective way to start--if you're not careful you can end up becoming a carbon copy of others instead of defining your individuality.

If you've ever seen the movie Finding Forrester, with Sean Connery and Rob Brown, you may remember a scene where Connery's character, William, sits the young writer, Jamal, in front of a typewriter and encourages him to just get writing. When Jamal doesn't know what to write, William encourages Jamal to copy something William had written. He hands Jamal a manuscript and says, "Start typing that. Sometimes the simple rhythm of typing gets us from page one to page two. And when you begin to feel your own words, start typing them."

It is OK to use what others have done before you as a jumping-off point for your own writing, but it's important to acknowledge where your heart starts taking over, and follow that path, instead of sticking to the one others have created. I should also mention that it's not OK to actually publish what you might have copied from someone else. Sure, you can use it as a tool to get your writing gears working, but you don't get to share that, at least not without expressed permission from the person you embellished.

Another way to go about finding your voice is to enlist a trusted friend in a fun experiment. This experiment will take some time and effort, but if you perform the following six-step process, I guarantee you'll be on your way to finding out who you are as a writer.

Step One

Take a friend out for coffee or, if you're really brave, cocktails. You want this person to know you well enough so that you can have a comfortable and casual conversation. This shouldn't been an acquaintance, someone you rarely speak to in person. It could be a friend, a sibling, a parent, or even a mentor.

Step Two

Place a voice recorder between you, on the table, and then have them ask you questions about the work you do. Even if they know everything about your work, have them ask you questions, as if it was the first time hearing about it. (This is critical.) They can be about why you do what you do, personal philosophy regarding the work itself, or even how to do certain parts of the work. The key is to get you talking at length about something you are passionate about.

Step Three
Take the recording home and listen to every single word closely. Do this two or three times. Listen to the points where you get excited, upset, anxious, and heated. You really want to get a sense of how your interest plays out in words when you're talking about them.

Step Four
Transcribe the entire conversation. Write down their questions, and then your answers. Do not edit! This isn't about being perfect, but getting the words down as you spoke them. Write down every blip, "um," and pregnant pause.

Step Five
Read the transcription out loud, as if you were reenacting the conversation, paying close attention to how you think you sound, and when the words you're reading start flowing from you as if you're reliving the conversation.

Step Six
Take what you've learned about yourself and write something else. Once you're done with that post, share it with your friend who helped you with the conversation. Ask them if it sounds like you. If they say "yes," then congratulate yourself. You're on the right path to finding your voice.

The trick here is to keep going. Don't let this experiment be wasted by inaction. Once you start to write, keep writing. The more you share, the more you will learn about your voice.

Finally, just like in real life, your voice is always changing. What you care about today may be different in a year, and much different in five years. Don't get bogged down by sticking to how you've always done things. Instead, focus on sharing what feels good to you, and what you feel your people need, right now.

Subjects Lines That Convert

There are many opinions on what makes a good subject line, and each expert will swear by their metrics that their strategy is the best. The one true statement you will hear from many of them is that only you will be able to accurately tell what works best for your readers. The problem being that you have to test your own theories often until you find what works. To help you with your experimentation, here are a few tips to consider.

Start with a conversation. If you consider the emails you get from friends, the conversational nature of those subject lines is usually a good start. Keep them short, perhaps pithy, and written like an informal sentence. You know how some email messages from marketers seem to be written in title case, with each word capitalized? Your friends don't send messages like that, and neither should you send them to your readers.

Some experts say that using the names of your readers in your subject line is a helpful way to get people's attention, and it might have been in the early days of data integration, but today's readers are savvy. They know that if you put their name in the message, that it's only because you extracted it from the information they have provided. There's nothing wrong with that, but it might appear to some readers like you're trying to portray your emails as personally written when they are smart enough to know otherwise.

Another technique is to use shocking or outlandish phrasing in a subject line, but I believe this approach should be used with caution. It's OK to use outlandish phrases in your emails that cause people to want to open your messages, but consider peppering it in once in a while instead of making it a permanent fixture in your approach.

If you're a reader of my newsletter, or a listener of my show, you know I'm not afraid to drop an F-bomb now and again. I once used the incredibly crass opener, "F**k this sh*t!" which I was a bit worried might scare people off. Thankfully, the readers appreciated my approach because that post still has the highest open rate of any email I had that year, almost 70%.

That email still shocked some, and I did lose a small contingent of readers, which hurt at first, but I knew if they couldn't handle that subject line, they probably couldn't handle much more of me. The reality is that most of my readers, even the most devout, wouldn't dig it if I came at them with email subject lines like that on a regular basis. So, yes, take a few opportunities to keep people guessing with your elusive, bold, or shocking subject line, but do so sparingly. Those notes keep the readers on the toes when they can't always guess where you're coming from, but too much and it becomes a gimmick that will wear them down.

When it comes to subject length, try to keep your subject lines to less than six words long. With mobile devices, the length of what shows up in a subject line is much smaller than what shows up in your native Gmail window. Because mobile is where a majority of people are viewing content these days, it's best to treat your notes with the expectation of that being where your readers are reading your stuff. If your email subject lines are much longer than five or six words, the core of your message is probably being chopped off, and may not make sense to the reader, especially if you aren't immediately qualifying the subject line within the first section of body copy. So, keep those titles short—shorter the better.

Also, avoid overused catch words like "free," "sale," or "open now." This will result in getting you marked as spam by the bots within email programs like Gmail, but they are also commonly overlooked by readers because they have seen those terms so often they're blinded to them. Be original and unique whenever possible, and talk to your people, not at them.

Finally, remain truthful at all costs. Even when I'm trying to shock people, or make them laugh with a subject line, the note still conveys the basic idea of the email. Never ever lie to your readers by telling them something to get them to open a message, then fail to deliver the content. This will make them lose trust in you faster than you can say, "The 10 Most Outlandish Things I Ever Told Anyone About Making Millions, Except Maybe You, [first name]."

There are lots of resources for how to write effective, attention-getting subjects that convert and sell. I've included some links in the Resources section of posts from people who are smarter than me on this subject, and I encourage you to read them all. I also encourage you to adapt their rules to fit your own reader needs. Again, this is not a one-size-fits-all situation. Use your instinct, but don't be afraid to take a chance once in a while.

4

Grow Your List

You may be wondering why it took me half a book to get to the whole point of the book in the first place—getting people on your list. I figured I needed to build up to a climax, and now here we are. Happy?

Let's start by asking a question. What do you think is the best way to get someone on your list? Is it by creating exclusive content that can't be found anywhere else but on your list? Is it by creating some sort of free resource or tutorial to entice them to join your list? Will you get more people to your list via your blog or your social media? Do sign-up forms work best at the top of the page or the bottom? How about the sidebar? And do pop-ups really work as well as everyone says they do?

The short answer to all those questions is, "It depends." There is no one right answer to this question, and you must consider several factors before you make your plan. Do you offer a product or service? Where do people find you most often, your blog, social media, or some other outlet? How do you like to provide for your fans and customers? Do you share your thoughts and ideas, or do you like to keep your musings to new offerings only? Do you have skills you can share that would help people? Is your social media approach weighted toward one site or app versus others?

Lots and lots of questions to ask and answer, but the beauty in this process is that you don't have to get it right on your first attempt. You don't have to get it right from your hundredth attempt, as long as you're learning new things as you go.

You also have two subscriber attraction possibilities to consider. First, you must have a sign-up form in place in order for them to join your list. From there, it's about finding the best way to attract them to that sign-up form. You could simply ask them to sign up and point them to a link, or you could provide something to them as a lead magnet, enticing them to join. There are mixed opinions about lead magnets. The opponents claim that anyone who signs up because of a free thing you provided isn't a true customer, because they were only invested in the list because you gave them something first. This is especially true if you are giving something away that isn't endemic of your products or services. Sure, you could get tons of people to sign up for your list by giving away a free iPad, but the kinds of people who would sign up are not likely folks who stick around, let alone buy from you.

As a proponent of lead magnets, I believe that if you're bringing people to your list, it's your job to give them something of value, at some time during their tenure as a subscriber, through the newsletter blasts you send. Why not put one of those value options right up front to show them what they can expect by being part of the list?

Throughout this next section, I'll break down some of the more popular lead magnet options, as well as some fringe ideas that people are experimenting with. I'll also talk about the different offerings I've given away, and what kind of success I had with them. To start, though, let's talk about the different ways of getting email addresses into a sign-up form.

Sign-up Forms

The complexity of a sign-up form can range from as little as a single box for an email address with a submit button, all the way to collecting vast amounts of demographic information. You can have people enter their website addresses, phone numbers, birthdays, age, sexual orientation, or whatever information you feel is pertinent to how you interact with your subscribers. Keep in mind, though, that with each new form field you add, you decrease the percentage of sign-ups a bit. Yeah, you can ask for their first child's name, but how many people are willing to put that information into the form of someone they don't know or trust yet?

All you really need is an email address, and maybe a first name. With that information alone, you can do a lot and not have to bother your readers for anything else except to ask for their attention. Many email service providers will extract some data from a subscribers' IP addresses to help you, like location, operating system they read on, browsers they use, and times of day they typically read. Yes, Big Brother is watching, but they're watching for your benefit this time, so it's OK.

We don't want to get too caught up in the types of information we capture. The tools we have at our disposal are secondary to making sure we provide value. Yes, I will pound that into your head repeatedly throughout this book, because it's really that important. Be aware of the tools you are provided by your email service as a way to serve your readers.

Placement and Frequency

Getting sign-up forms onto a website a decade ago was something left for the coders. Embedding a code into a WordPress template was not for the faint of heart, or those naive of JavaScript. On my first attempt at a blog, I tried to embed a code with virtually no success. Instead of getting a code monkey to help, I gave up, relenting until the development of more robust plugins and third-party apps.

Today, putting a sign-up on your site is simple, no matter what platform you use. Some services like Squarespace have automatic integration with email providers like Mailchimp, and can build a form on the page for you in a couple clicks. People getting started now have it much easier, which means absolutely no excuses for not having a sign-up form available for people.

The more complex question then becomes where to place it, and how many you should have. This is a hotly debated conversation, with a variety of opinions. There is no one right answer for everyone. Also, because technology is always changing, as is the way people consume it, the best answer for you will change over time. My opinion is that you should have several options in various places, represented in various ways, because no two people read through your website the same way.

At the time of this writing, on my site, Fresh Rag, I have three potential opt-in opportunities above the fold* (the space visible from a browser window when they first arrive). If someone clicks through to one of my posts and scrolls all the way to the bottom, there are as many as seven ways they can get onto my list, and none of them look the same.

Some time ago, Derek Halpern of Social Triggers wrote, "The 7 High-Converting Places to Add Email Sign-Up Forms to Build Your †List." That post was written back when the standard layout for a blog was a large column for main content, and a sidebar for links, buttons, and advertising. Regarded as one of the leaders of list-building knowledge, Halpern has since changed his website to focus on a more mobile-friendly design, but his list of high-converting places still stands strong, and are as follows.

---

* "Above the fold," is a term carried over from the newspapers industry, which refers to any content that resides on the first half of the front page of the newspaper, which what was visible from newsstands. You would have to flip the paper over to see what was below the fold.

† Derek Halpern - The 7 high-converting places to add email sign-up forms to build your list - Social Triggers:
http://socialtriggers.com/email-sign-up-forms-build-list/

- The Feature Box: The space at the top of your site, adjacent to your logo or nameplate, readily visible and up front. If you go to his site now, you can't miss his feature box
- Top of Sidebar: If you have a sidebar, the first thing in that sidebar should be an opt-in
- After Single Post: Each blog post is a web page unto itself. If people are reading to the bottom, they rarely scroll back up to remember to sign up. Capture them as they are done reading.
- Site Footer: If people scroll past your content, through your comments, and down to your footer, give them another chance to sign up before they go back to the top, or bounce off your site.
- About Page: Aside from your home page, the second most popular page on your site will almost always be your About page, because people want to know more about the person whose site they are visiting. Let them find out more about you, and then get their email address.
- Header Bar: You've probably seen some sites that have a small sliver of a bar at the very top of the their site, maybe leading to special content. These typically lead to a form. Sometimes they are a form unto themselves.
- Pop-Ups: Goes without saying, the pop-up box still remains one of the most effective ways to get people on your list.

This doesn't mean you have to put sign-up forms in all these places, and you don't need to have as many as I do, but you may want to try out a few different options and see which ones work best for you. I've seen a lot of small-business owners take a passive approach to forms because they are afraid of annoying readers. This can be a valid point, depending on your specific readers, but I'm willing to bet most readers will be less annoyed by repeated opt-in opportunities if those opportunities are presented in a way that makes them unique, and of course, valuable.

One other thing to consider is if your site is more about selling product, and there's less sharing of information, then perhaps fewer opt-in boxes is best. However, if your blog is chock-full of free information, You've earned the right to share as many opt-ins as you want. You don't have to take all the opportunities, but you're giving your knowledge away freely, so why not give people a chance to get more of that in email form?

The Dreaded Pop-Up
Love them or hate them, pop-ups are a fact of our business life, and instead of writing them off completely, it's best to consider all the possibilities before

counting them out. If you do a search on Google for the phrase, "Do pop-ups work," you'll get back hundreds of links to blog posts by prominent marketers all sharing the same basic sentiment: Pop-ups work.

Are they annoying to some people? Yes, but instead of treating annoyance as an all-or-nothing metric, look at it as varying degrees of annoyance. I have pop-ups on my site, and I'll talk about how I use them in my strategy section later, but I openly admit that I get annoyed by some pop-ups on other sites. However, most pop-ups are not so annoying that they make me bounce from a site. In fact, the annoyance comes mostly from my desire to consume whatever content I went to the site for in the first place. For me, pop-ups are rarely a deal breaker.

Although I may click past an pop-up, one thing it tells me in an instant is that the site has a newsletter. Even if I don't sign up via the pop-up, if the content is solid and valuable, I may find myself seeking out another form on the page (provided they have done their due diligence and offered more than one opt-in opportunity). I may not have considered the newsletter option otherwise.

Another thing to consider with pop-ups is that not all are created equally. Some pop-ups can be a real pain in the butt if they're difficult to click away from. Others will pop up with every page you visit, and some will pop up even after you've already signed up for a site's list. The technology of pop-ups has changed a lot over the past few years, making them more dynamic and interesting, as well as intelligent. It's now easy for even the most inexperienced blogger to implement a pop-up that not only knows the person visiting the page, but knows when they last visited, and cross-checks if they are already on a list. Pop-ups can now serve different purposes depending on the visiting patterns of people, delivering different information based on where someone came from or where they are going. They also come with statistics that allow you to see what works best, where you should place them, or when you might want to remove them.

If you have a lot of people bailing on your site after a certain pop-up, then you know you need to fix something. The level of annoyance is dictated by your visitors, but luckily, it's adjusted on the fly by you. If you use this information to your advantage, you can make pop-ups work in your favor. Remember to keep in mind that your site's visitors will likely be less disturbed by a pop-up than you imagine. Test and tune your pop-ups, and then decide when you have real information in your hands.

Get Magnetic
Marketing on the Internet is a tricky thing. As soon as a new social media app comes out, there's already thousands of marketers on the platform

trying to exploit it. At the time of this writing, the live video app, Periscope, is gaining a lot of ground, and because of that, there are marketers all over it. Instead of the early days of Twitter and Facebook, where people weren't sure what to do on those platforms, and therefore acted human, there are lots of marketers on Periscope talking about how to win at Periscope. The platform isn't even six months old and there's already would-be gurus lining up to take the mantle of renowned expert.

In his chat at the Inc. 500 Conference in 2013, Gary Vaynerchuk[*] (a marketer) talks about how people are mismanaging their influence by constantly hitting people in the face with what he refers to as right hooks. Instead of repeatedly jabbing content that delivers quality, these marketer always swing for a knock-out punch. "Marketers ruin everything," is a mantra Vaynerchuk uses often in his talks around the world, and no matter how many times he says it, the status quo won't be changing anytime soon. Unsurprisingly, those marketers who are constantly trying to push sales at people are the ones who get ignored first.

The biggest problem for us, as small-business owners just trying to eke out a living is that we are competing against these big-dog marketers who ruin everything. And because they ruin it, that makes our job tougher. No matter how authentic and straightforward we want to be, the level of trust with consumers is low, right from the start. So we are taxed with the responsibility of bringing high-quality value to the people right out of the gate, almost as penance for the actions of all the marketers who came before us. They made a mess, and now we have to deal with the aftermath.

The reason I bring this up is because you are going to struggle to get people to join your list, not because they don't like you, but because people are jaded and don't trust easily. They have been scammed and spammed consistently for years, and getting them to give up that precious space in their inbox takes some convincing.

The use of lead magnets (anything you might provide for free in order to get people to sign up for your email list), is something that not everyone is comfortable with. Even some of the most savvy marketers and business owners do not believe that you need to give anything away for free in order to get people to sign up. The thing is, everyone who runs a list is already giving something away for free.

Whether you're giving away a free PDF guide right as someone joins your list, or you're giving free tips each week in your newsletter, you're

---

[*]   Inc. 500 Conference with Gary Vaynerchuk, 2013 (video). The irony of this link is that you will likely be hit by both a pop-up ad, and an ad in the video screen before you can watch Gary.
http://www.inc.com/gary-vaynerchuk/marketers-ruin-everything.html

still always giving something away free. The difference being that the person who didn't give away a freebie at the start was either much more persuasive in getting people on their list, or they aren't getting the same amount of sign-ups as someone who did.

Take a moment to think about the different newsletters you've signed up for in the past. There were probably some you jumped on because they gave something away, so ask yourself what it was about that thing they offered that caused you to join? What was the value proposition they gave in exchange for your email address? How can you leverage that idea for yourself?

Now think about the times you've joined a list without a bonus. What compelled you to take the leap of faith that you would be getting value from the trade? Was it the person's status, or the quality of their already free content? Was it some promise of cooler things within the confines of the email newsletter that hooked you? Something about that situation provided you enough trust of the individual or company to make handing over your email a no-brainer. Can you use that idea in your own process of enlisting subscribers?

On my site, I use varying strategies with my sign-up opportunities. Some of my opt-ins talk about a freebie, and others merely talk about getting tips, news and special offers delivered to them when they join. Looking at my analytics, it's clear that the opt-ins with the free ebook offer get the most attention. However, I am an information marketer (yeah, the ones that ruin everything) and this model works for me. You must judge for yourself--and for your fans--if giving something away is valuable and worthwhile.

Popular Lead Magnet Options

What you offer as a way to get people on your list is only limited by your own imagination. I know this because I see new lead magnet ideas popping up all the time. However, there are some core standards.

I'm sure there are people in your market who offer up something to their subscribers. It's not a terrible idea to look at what those others are doing and use it as inspiration, but without copying. Put your own spin on things, and differentiate.

To get you thinking about options, here are a few of the more popular ways people provide content to attract subscribers. Take these ideas and expand on them, or dig deep and see how you can make something truly unique. Perhaps it's a meld of two or more ideas. Remember, no rules, so don't be afraid to get creative.

Consistent Delivery

I have a friend who is a illustrator with a wicked-dark sense of humor. She shares cartoons on her blog on a regular basis, and to attract new subscribers, she offers them an exclusive comic strip if they sign up for her list, and she never shares that cartoon with anyone outside her list. Of course, the readers share her cartoons all the time, but she doesn't get worked up about it. Each cartoon is marked with a URL that directs people back to her website, which hopefully leads to more people signing up for her list.

The real genius of this strategy is that you get a new comic strip delivered to your inbox free each week, but it's not really new. If you sign up today, you'll get the same email I got when I signed up two weeks ago, and the one that I'm getting this week, you will get in two more weeks. She's using the power of automation to her advantage. She doesn't have to continually add to the content each week, but instead lets the technology do the work for her. People who sign up in a year from now may still get the same content, but also have an entire year of free content sent to them, and the artist can sit back and watch it happen. She still draws new comics each week, but if she had to skip a week or two, her readers at the front of the line would wait patiently for her next piece because she's delivered so much awesomeness week in and week out.

If you're an illustrator, an artist, a photographer, or some other visual creative, you could do the same. If you're an author, a poet, a lifestyle blogger, perhaps offer tidbits in a drip feed that people get depending on when they sign up.

Ebook/Guide

Originally I had this section titled as PDF, because in the past, most of this content was delivered in a PDF format, but it doesn't have to be. All of your opt-in freebie information could be posted on a single blog page that you hide from public view. You can password-protect it if you want, or keep it open but make it unavailable to search engines by marking the page as "no index." This tells web crawlers from Google and other search engines that the page they are looking at doesn't really exist, and the search engine should not index it for their resource. That way nobody stumbles upon your lead magnet content by accident.

Of course you can make it an actual PDF, and that way people can download it, and print it out if they want, but it's not a necessity anymore. Instead of them printing it, you could encourage them to bookmark the link for future reference. Again, no rules here, but if you do put it on your website, make sure you plan on keeping it there for awhile. If you're wondering what to write about, below are a few ideas within the ebook/

guide category you might consider.

How-Tos

If you have a unique skill or technique that you use in your work or business, you could create a how-to guide to help others do what you do. Maybe you have a blogging technique that helps you stay focused and on schedule with your posts. If you're a knitter, it could be a trade-secret tip that shows people how to do something complicated that you've found but not many others do.

Anything that you can imagine teaching someone else to do is something you could share. Also, even if you feel like you don't have enough to share, remember that there are people not as far down the path as you, and they would love to know some of the secrets you've shared. You don't have to break down barriers with your content, but rather share your world with someone just reaching the level you've been for awhile. Not only does this solidify your position as an authority, but you've built up a tremendous amount of good will with that person.

Top Ten Lists

This concept is simple; compile a list of things that will help your reader achieve something. It could be your ten best tools, ten online resources you use, or ten people to follow on Twitter who will change their life. The subject can be anything, as long as it's appealing and will help your readers in some way.

I say ten, but this could be any number, as long as the number communicates an appropriate amount of value. That said, ten is a nice round number that is common enough to be inviting to people. Nine or less just doesn't have the same oomph.

Niche Insights

Let's say you've been doing your work for a decent amount of time, and in that period, you've learned some tips and tricks that most people don't talk about. It could be the way you manage your studio or office, how to operate in an online marketplace, or the best ways to use social media for your niche. You have specific knowledge in your area that other people who want to do what you do will never learn unless they spend the time doing it. Why not tell them? Save them time and money, and you'll be their hero for life.

Cheat Sheets

Are you good with spreadsheets? I'm not, but I know people who are, and some of these crafty types have come up with ways to use spreadsheets to manage their business. They make inventory tracking sheets, pricing metrics, social media stat trackers, and all kinds of other things that help them.

The cheat sheet you produce doesn't have to be a spreadsheet, either. It could be a list of terms for newbies, measurements converted for certain types of work. A pile of links to different useful sites, or a bunch of popular hashtags for your industry.

My friend Danielle Spurge of MeriweatherCouncil.com published a free list of ten creative hashtags for Instagram on her blog. At the end of the post, she had a link for people to get ten more, which took them to a sign-up form for her list. I'm sure you're familiar with the phrase, "hook, line, and sinker."

Product Samples

This approach works best for people who produce digital content, because the information is easy to distribute. If you are a maker of physical things, then you're not likely to send out a sample of your stuff to everyone who signed up for your newsletter. On the other hand, if you work in pixels and code, then you probably have something cool to share.

Templates

If you're a designer who knows how to make templates that average individuals need, why not share some? Whether it's Photoshop, Illustrator, InDesign, or whatever creative program you work in, if you create a few common templates, people will clamor to get them.

Photoshop Goodies

I recently joined a list of a graphic artist who sells loads of digital product on CreativeMarket.com, an online shop for design products. Joining his list, I got some of his free Photoshop ready textures, Photoshop actions, and a typeface. He sends out email blasts about twice a week, and it's usually to share that he's got a deal on one of his packages for sale, but every once in a while he'll toss a new goodie. Since he's making them for his business anyway, he might as well skim off a few to keep the people happy.

Books

If you're an author, you can easily distribute your books to people through your newsletter. You could give them a sample chapter of the book just for signing up. At the end of the chapter, you have a link to the whole book, which will hopefully make some sales for you. Another way I've seen this done is to distribute a book, one chapter at a time over several weeks. You send them one chapter per message, and if they want the whole thing, they have to stick around to the end to get it, or buy it with the link you share at the bottom. Meanwhile, they're on your list, gaining trust in you with each chapter they read.

Starter Packs

Another friend of mine makes downloadable packs for parents who homeschool their kids. To get people on her list, she has various starter packs available for people to get. Depending on where they stumbled across her website and what page they visited, new readers can get one of the various downloads for free. She also sweetens the deal once they're in by giving them more, and will share some throughout the year, but there are always links to the products she sells.

Download of the Month

If you're not familiar with Death to Stock (deathtostockphoto.com, you should be. It's a stock photography site run by a couple of professional photographers who specialize in atypical stock images, not the cliché crap you see in most stock agencies. Sign up for their email list and they will send you a bunch of high-resolution images each month for free. The catch is you're not supposed to use them for commercial reasons, and you're supposed to give credit to Death to Stock, but you can always buy a license for the images for a small fee. I'm a subscriber, and this is one of the emails I look forward to getting each month. I have seen artists and illustrators do this with wallpapers, calendar pages, or other downloadables. They repurpose a design they've already made, and turn it into a download for readers each month. It's a simple, resourceful idea, and keeps the people happy.

Videos

This is a bit more complex than the others, and a bigger investment in your time, but the reward for offering a video, or series of videos, can be huge numbers of people signing up for your list. Go above and beyond what other people are providing as a lead magnet and you will get massive turnout. You don't have to go too nuts, one to three videos on a given topic or theme. The number of the videos is less important than the value you give people, but from a consumer standpoint, three is much cooler than one.

The beauty of video is that it humanizes you to them more, which means more trust. More trust means more sales, and more sharing of your content with others. One pro tip is to keep videos under ten minutes each, because it's less work for you and also keeps their attention. Longer than that and the content becomes less interesting. Keep them jazzed by giving them more videos at a shorter length.

How-To Videos

Find a topic to share that is detailed enough to turn into a few short videos that help people do something. It could be a series that gets them through one particular project, or it could be a short series of novice, intermediate, and advanced techniques around a single theme. You could deliver them all at once, or over a few separate emails, each giving you an opportunity to promote something to them. Maybe you have a training series for sale that coincides, or you have some product templates for them to purchase that will make their own jobs easier. Making videos that show them in action make for a huge selling opportunity.

Monologue

Are you the type who likes to share intimate things with strangers? I know a few people like this, and they spend a lot of time on video talking to their viewers, telling them about their life experiences. As a matter of fact, I could be one of them, but that's as much as I'll say. You'll have to do your own research to find out more.

You could put together a series of videos where each one talks about your own professional journey, including any discoveries you've made along the way about your work. Share your personal highs and lows, tie them back into your work, and people will love you for sharing.

Interviews

If you have close relationships with other people in your field, perhaps consider getting together with them and filming a conversation, allowing them to shed some insight into the work, or just tell some funny or inspirational stories. You can do this in person or with video calling through Skype or Google Hangout. Of all the above options, this is probably the easiest to accomplish, unless you don't know anyone. If that's the case, go hang out with people in your niche. You'll be better for it, and you might make some new friends or, better, partners in crime.

Riding the Fringe

The above ideas are the most common options, but they can also be commonplace. If you'd like to step into areas that most in your industry won't touch, here are a few more advanced or robust options to consider as lead magnets for your list.

Free Webinar

The approach to this would be similar to video, except instead of the videos being constantly available, joining the webinar would be for a limited time only. This means you only have certain windows to get people on your list, but it creates a sense of scarcity within people. They won't want to miss out on the chance to see the webinar, especially if you make it super awesome.

You could take the same video models above (how-to, monologue, or interviews) and turn them into a webinar. Depending on which service you would use to present the webinar, an added bonus over video is that you could answer questions from your audience, live. You could also bring people into the call to interact with you and/or your guest.

Webinar services range in price between free and hundreds of dollars, depending on your needs, usually dictated by how many people you want to invite to watch, how robust you want the interactivity to be, and if you want to charge people for viewing. I've used Google Hangouts On Air as a webinar service, and it worked great for a one-time offering. It's entirely up to you how you want to manage it, but you get what you pay for. Free means you're going to be doing all the legwork yourself, and the paid options will obviously make your life a little easier in getting the technology to work together. Just remember the goal is to provide value. If you drop the ball on that, people will bounce, then leave your list disgruntled--and perhaps head to Twitter to rant about their disappointment.

If you want to know how successful webinars are run, I suggest finding people who do them well, then emulate those people. Amy Porterfield, Lewis Howes, and John Lee Dumas are three marketers who own this medium, but there are many to choose from. Watch how others do it, and then bring the thunder in your own way.

Challenge Campaign

I've touched on drip campaigns a little, where you use automation to deliver a series of emails over a given amount of time, anywhere from a couple days, to keeping people engaged for weeks or months. Usually, drip campaigns are put together using content you've already created, which allows you to share evergreen* information with people, in succession, no matter when they sign up. This makes your job easier because you don't have to worry which readers have seen what posts, because they're going to get all of them eventually, if they stay enrolled.

A challenge campaign is taking this concept a bit further. Instead of just sending out a few scheduled messages to new enrollees, you're sending them down a daily path of emails focused on achieving something specific. For instance, my Creative Badass Challenge is a month-long series of emails, one delivered each day with a specific purpose, and all of them geared toward a goal. The emails are the lead magnet, and people join by the handfuls every day. When people finish the challenge, I migrate them over to my main mailing list, and they start receiving my regular drip campaign.

I have other friends who run challenges for list building, learning how to make videos, writing consistently, improving their phone photography, and a bunch of other ideas. The one thing to keep in mind is that these challenges are very intensive to implement. You will also need to upgrade your Mailchimp account, or have a service provider that allows automation, to make this work. Most providers do have it, but it's usually a paid service. That said, with a challenge, you're putting yourself in people's inboxes on a consistent basis, with the added benefit of an option for them to buy something you're selling within each email. So while you may have to pay for the service, you're hopefully making up for it by selling something.

Street Team

The idea of hosting a street team has been around for awhile, but it's getting a resurgence lately. I personally have never run a group of dedicated fans in a street team, but I am considering the idea, especially as a way to get my books into higher rankings on the different platforms. By the time you read this chapter, I may have already implemented my plan to use a street team to my advantage.

A street team is not like your regular list of subscribers, but instead an elite squad that you pull together to help you test your products or services, spread the word about your work, and help you grow your business. Why would anyone want to do this for you? Free stuff, of course.

The way I see it working for me is I put a call to action out to my

---

*   Something that is evergreen stands strong for a long period of time. Evergreen content doesn't go stale quickly, but continues to be relevant for years.

current list of subscribers. I tell them I'm building a street team of hardcore fans who want to help me promote and share. In exchange, they will be active readers of my work, and get everything I produce at no cost to them. If I put out a book, they get a free copy. In exchange, I expect them to read it and give me feedback. I also expect them to go to the various channels to leave a trusted and honest review. As long as they don't harpoon me, I don't care what they write (hopefully it's positive), as long as they do it. Anyone who doesn't make the commitment gets removed from the team,

If you do this right, you don't need a lot of members on your team. You could have as few as twenty dedicated people who are willing to help you promote and share your work. This works best for information-based businesses, services, or digital products, but also has some applications within product-based business. Brainstorm the idea, and I'm sure you could come up with a way to entice a team of people to have your back consistently.

Again, having to mail a special thing you produce out to your street team every time you make something new would be an expensive undertaking, and perhaps cost prohibitive. Still, you might be able to find a way to attract these ravenous and dedicated fans.

Those are just a few ideas to get you started with lead magnets, but I bet you could come up with dozens of ideas on your own. Crack open a note pad, peruse the web for what other people are offering, and jot down any random ideas that come to you. Don't worry about their validity yet, just write them down. You can figure out which one is the best idea later.

Not every idea is meant for all people. Some are better than others, so I recommend you do some research first about what your people want. Once you have a clear idea of a gap in the market, you can fill that gap with your content and implement it, but do a little local research first to find out what your viewers are interested in. This will save you a lot of heartache and headache, because you don't want to slave away on a project that may not sell. Asking your tribe first is always a good plan.

Social Media for Sign-ups

Because much of our promotional time is being spent on social media these days, it seems natural to talk about our email list respective to these social spaces. Keeping in mind our balance between giving value and asking for attention, social media can be an effective tool for bringing people into the fold. Bear in mind that these sites and apps are still meant to be social places, not for blasting your content in people's faces 100% of the time.

With each platform listed below, there are both subtle and direct ways to draw people's attention to your sign-up form, By mixing up the techniques, with a little experimentation and a ton of generosity, you'll get people jumping onto your list. Take these techniques in, play around, and focus on the ones that work best. I'm only going into the bigger players in the social space because this is where you'll likely find the bulk of your readers. If there is a space where you connect with a lot of your fans and customers that I haven't included, take into consideration the things discussed here and see how you can apply them to your preferred network.

Facebook

The power of organic reach in Facebook has diminished greatly, and it's possible much of your promotional energy might be better spent elsewhere, but Facebook has made some recent concessions to business page owners that might help get you some readers.

The pinned posts on your business page are the first option you should be using to your advantage. If you're not familiar with pinned posts, you simply craft a post that sends people to a link on your site where they can sign up for your list. Once you publish the post, click the dropdown arrow on the upper right side of the post, and click the Pin to Top option. This will make that post stick to the top of your page's feed no matter what you post afterward.

What I personally have found to be the most effective way of making this work is to link from Facebook to a blog post that provides a lot of value, and has at least one interesting graphic that shows up in Facebook when you post the link. You want people to click through, then read your post, so you can get them to your sign-up box at the bottom of the blog post, or perhaps with a pop-up. You could also craft a blog post that centers around your lead magnet. That way you get them curious about the subject, and let them know they can get more if they sign up.

If you go to my page right now (ww.facebook.com/freshrag), and look at my cover image, it's most likely doing three things. First, the image I use almost always illustrates my latest lead magnet. Second, if you happen to click that image, the description will have a link that takes you to my opt-in page. Third, there will be something within the graphic that subtly (or not so subtly) points to the call-to-action button at the top of the page, within the header. If people click that call-to-action button, it will take them direct to information about my lead magnet. If you're not using the call to action button yet, you need to get on that. 80% of my sign-ups through Facebook come through that button. You may have different success, but it's a highly visible, effortless, and free way to get people to your sign-up form. Why wouldn't you take advantage of that?

Facebook obviously allows you to link to your website on your page. Instead of linking directly to your homepage, though, you could adjust the link to point toward your opt-in page, or at least your most popular content that also has a sign-up form within it. Doing this increases your chances of getting someone on your list far more than sending them blindly to your homepage. Sure, if someone finds your homepage, there is a chance they could get to a sign-up form, but then you're asking them to potentially take more clicks to get there. Each extra click you add between them and your sign-up form is another chance for them to bail off your site without taking the action you had hoped they might.

One other option I've been using a lot lately is to upload video content instead of plain text messages or photos. The videos get way more engagement than the other options, and with each video you post, Facebook gives you the option of a call to action at the end of the video. This is a highly effective tool that I've only recently started taking advantage of, but I'm seeing big returns on it whenever I post a video. If you're bullish on video, I highly recommend using them more often than other post options.

Outside of business pages, the best way I've found to get people interested in joining my list is through my private groups. I have one called the Fresh Rag Army that's free to anyone who wants to join, and it's filled with lots of creative individuals willing to help each other out. Managing a group takes more time and energy, because you have to foster a community around something you're doing, but if done right, you build trust, and you can occasionally ask people to join your list.

The beauty of groups is that you are likely going to attract people with mutual interests, so they are more likely to want to hear from you, rather than random folks who know nothing about you. Not everyone will be able to build a group around their specific work, but consider building one around the niche you serve. You'll want to make it niche (Stay-at-home moms who knit), but not too niched (stay-at-home moms from Peoria, Illinois, who knit and drive Subarus). Once you have your niche picked, invite all your friends to join in the fun, and moderate as you see fit.

Twitter

If there was ever a platform to use the model of give, give, give, ask, Twitter is that platform. Whenever you step into this place, keep in mind that Twitter has become less about social interaction and more about sharing information. Yes, social still exists, but in comparison, your Twitter feed is more about things that are happening right now with everyone, whether that's news or their latest blog post. You still have the capacity to share your stuff there, obviously, but this is not the place to be knocking every pitch into the grandstand. Twitter should not be treated like a home run derby.

I have personally taken on a 10:1 ratio of give to ask. For me, I think it's beneficial to present myself as a trusted source of information first, gaining the trust of others, before I hit them over the head with my stuff. Granted, my gives can oftentimes be my own content, but this is the stuff I give away freely, like blog posts and podcast episodes. I consider the asks anything where someone has to give me something other than their attention, whether that's money or an email address.

Now, when you're in ask mode, and you're ready to share your email opt-in or lead magnet with people, try to craft a tweet that will capture attention and get people to favorite, retweet, and click through. Then when you're done, just like in your Facebook feed, pin that tweet to the top. One thing to note is that you want that tweet to be as evergreen as possible. That way you can leave it up there for a reasonable amount of time, hopefully bringing people to your opt-in. Of course, you could craft a new tweet on a regular basis and swap it out, which doesn't take much time to do, but in case you forget to do so, might as well make that tweet sustainable.

Also like Facebook, you have an opportunity to share your website address in your profile. Make sure to point it to your opt-in page.

Pinterest

Just like the others, you have a link to your website in your profile. Use it wisely, and point people exactly where you want them to go. Yes, I am going to repeat this with each one on this list, just to hammer that idea home.

You should have pins that point to your opt-in and/or core content, which is perfectly acceptable, as long as you don't inundate people with them. The best way I've seen this done is by creating multiple visuals that take quotes or bits of information directly from the core content itself. You either grab the images from within the post, or you upload a brand-new pin, and then link it back to your content or opt-in page. Depending on the depth of your content or lead magnet, you could create several, if not dozens of branded graphics that point back to that one post. The more interesting the pin, the more likely it will get liked and repinned. Depending on how many graphics you create, I recommend trickling them in over time, maybe one or two a day. Make the river of information flow for a good, long time, and pepper the posts in with other pins that you share, so the top of your feed doesn't make you look like a self-absorbed mess.

Having a board specifically set up for this content is also a good idea, and each post gets put into this board. I recommend you maintain transparency here, and within the description of the board, make sure you let people know it's a collection of your musings around your own content. You can add a link to that opt-in page in the description, and then let people figure out the rest on their own. If you build this board and make it so people have no idea that all the pins in the board lead to the same page or pages, you might lose credibility with some folks.

Instagram

Oh, how I love Instagram. This has become my favorite social media app since I started using it with purpose. That right there is a big clue to how to make Instagram work for you—go in with purpose. If you visit my account (instagram.com/freshrag), you'll see that I'm doing my best to create a theme. Instead of sharing the same types of pictures, or the same subject matter as other popular Insta-celebs, I maintain a visual order to things that has a unique aesthetic.

I use a black, white, and gold palette straight from my site's branding, and also checkerboard pattern to add visual interest. I wanted to have one of those highly curated accounts that looked consistent and beautiful from one image to the next, but because I share such random things in my photos, it was hard to maintain a look. Instead, I forced a look onto the images that I was posting, and now I get lots of comments from people telling me how much they like the look of my feed.

How does any of this help me get people to sign up for my newsletter? Trust! Because I'm building a consistent theme with my images, one that resembles the look of all my branding, it gives people visual comfort, and when their comfortable, they let down their guard just enough to listen to what I have to say. When I post something up about a new lead magnet I have, people pay attention.

If trust is built with sharing valuable content, then the value on Instagram is provided in the cohesiveness of your images. If you're all herky-jerky with your images, style, and branding, people will be less inclined to pay attention for long.

If you have your images in check, then you can focus on getting viewers to your site, as with the other sites, make sure to point people to your opt-in page. Repetitive or not, still make it a priority. Within Instagram, there's only one place people can get from your account to your content with a single click, so make sure you take advantage of that by sending them to the best stuff first.

Just like Pinterest, you can create graphics emblematic of your content that you can share through Instagram, as long as the images you shared on Pinterest are also aligned with your style and branding on Instagram. You could always create the graphics for Instagram, and then send those posts over to Pinterest via IFTTT instead, but the flow of content is completely up to you.

If you're posting something that is meant to point to specific content to get people signed up, then I recommend you put a link in your description, and do it within the first hundred characters. I'll explain the reasoning behind this later when I talk about repurposing content, but the gist is that you want that link to translate when you push the image to other platforms, even if that link isn't clickable in Instagram.

If there was any downside to Instagram, it's that linking out anywhere beyond your profile is unsupported. You can post links in your photo descriptions all you want, but inexplicably, Instagram has made it so people cannot copy the text within a post. I understand keeps insidious links at bay, but it makes our jobs a lot harder, especially if we're trying to encourage people to share our work with others. In the grand scheme of our promotional efforts, this is a small issue, and I'll tell you about my work-around later.

YouTube

If video is your thing, this will be a good opportunity to make a big impact, because when it comes to building trust with people, it's hard to beat video. As long as you bring value and are entertaining, people will form an instant affinity toward you, because you're right there, talking to them. A five-minute video you share on YouTube can have a much bigger impact on someone than a thousand-word blog post, or dozens of tweets, posts, and pinned images.

If you're using videos within whatever opt-in page you're creating, or within your core content, you should make sure your descriptions for those videos have links back to your content from within YouTube. It's also a good idea to keep that information within the first couple lines so it doesn't get cut off behind the "Show More" button. Keeping it above that line will ensure the link is visible no matter where someone sees it.

Something I'm just now getting into with some of my YouTube videos is the card function, where I have the option of sharing clickable information in a visual card that pops up exactly when I want it. Cards can be a bit intrusive once clicked, because they cover a reasonable amount of the screen area, but if you time them right, they're a powerful way to get people to take action.

Annotations are similar to cards, but instead of being an expandable tabs, these come in the form of hot spots or speech bubbles that appear at certain times during the video. You get to control the size of the clickable area, the length they are visible, and where they point. The popular method for implementing annotations is to incorporate some sort of visual into your video edit, and then use the hot spot option to add a clickable area around the graphics in the video. It goes without saying that you should only be putting links in the annotations that make sense to the content of the video. If the video doesn't talk about your newsletter or lead magnet, you could always add a spot in the video at the end that talks about those things. By splicing in a closing call to action at the end, you're able to stick to the content, and then when it's appropriate, link to the opt-in.

Of course you know the part about having links in your profile that go to your sign-up form.

Periscope

Live video has been around for awhile, but it's getting a resurgence, and the rules have yet to be written on the social standard for these areas. I believe it's too early to tell what the ideal length of live video should be, how often you should be doing them, or what types of content people like to consume in this space. It's an Oklahoman land rush for any possible opportunity to gain new followers, so how do we use this as a way to get people onto our lists?

That's a good question, and one to which I'm going to repeat the tenets of value, trust, and to always coming to the table from a place of helping others. Do that, and no matter what the rules end up being, you'll always be on the right side of the line. Now, let's use that idea and get some people on your list.

First, something to keep in mind with Periscope, and other apps like it (Meerkat, StreamMe, Snapchat), is that the content has a limited shelf life. Periscope recordings can only be made available for 24 hours. After that they are deprecated, lost to the ether. As the content creator though, you have the opportunity to save all your broadcasts as videos to use in other places. I personally save each Periscope broadcast as a habit because I may want to repurpose the content to share on other platforms like YouTube and Facebook.

My friend Steph Gaudreau from StupidEasyPaleo.com recently launched a new training program for her fans. She's also using Periscope a lot, and having a blast doing it. I asked her how she planned on using Periscope to get people on her list, and she told me her plan to do a succession of daily videos, all in a specific order. At some point during each video, she references her new program and then shares a link to her opt-in page. Since she can't write anything to share with people during the video, what she does is writes the URL on a small notepad, which she can hold up for the camera. People can read it or do a screen shot to collect the URL for later use. She also encourages at least one person in the group to share the link in a comment so it gets referenced repeatedly.

To take that idea one step further, my friend Holly Gillen of HollyGStudios.com is taking her Periscope videos and uploading them direct to YouTube. If your content is genuinely badass (as it should be, because why would you share anything less?), why not share it with others in a more long-term platform. Of course, you do all the normal YouTubey things above to make it worthwhile. I've started this myself, and taken it a step further by posting the videos on Facebook to maximize my exposure.

Because you don't have a lot of opportunity to share an active link within the Periscope platform, the best advice I can give is to go into Periscope with a clear plan of what you want to share. Use content that you craft to entice people to your sign-up form. If you've already broken down the content, as you might in other platforms, use that plan, but with the added bonus of showing your human side.

YouTube allows you to show your voice and personality. Periscope allows you to share your humanity. When filming, be sure to interact and engage people. Thank them for joining, answer their questions, give some a shout-out, and then ask them to share you with others. If you're doing good work there, they will do this for you.

There's also the profile link thing. Do that too.

One last thing to note is that Periscope has taken an early lead in this live video arena due to it's affiliation with Twitter. Meerkat is right on their heels though, and even while I wrote this book, Facebook officially announced it's own live video service called Mentions. The shootout for dominance in this space has only just begun, so you may not want to hitch your wagon to any one platform just yet. Experiment with each, find your groove, and grow your following. When the dust settles on who took the lead with live video, you'll either be in good standing where you are, or you can try to migrate people over to another platform.

Commenting, Contributing, and Sharing

You should be well aware of those three words and how they work with social media. Another three words you should be familiar with are "know, like, and trust," as they coincide well with the first three. If you want people to know, like, and trust you, then you will need to move beyond posting stuff online that revolves around you, and start commenting, contributing, and sharing. Seems like a no-brainer, right? Unfortunately, not so much.

Many times we get so caught up in making stuff happen for our own work that we forget the social aspect of social media, but this is where you hurt your brand the most. You can post up all the pretty pictures you want on Instagram, and yes, you're going to gain followers, but if you ever want them to truly believe in you, then you need to partake in the conversation. When people comment on your posts, reply to them. When you see something online that you dig, make sure you let them know. If it's super awesome, share it with others. I know this sounds like rudimentary learning, but it's not as common as you might think.

I have an experiment for you. Go to Twitter right now and count the first twenty tweets in your stream. Now, how many of them are links to outside content? Specifically, how many are links to the content of the person sharing it? How many are retweets? How many of those retweets did someone add their own message to showing thanks or appreciation for the first post? How many are using popular hashtags in their tweets just to make themselves more visible? Finally, how many of those tweets are just people trying to be conversational, sharing random thoughts? Random quotes from famous people do not count.

When I was a teenager, the '80s were commonly referred to as the me generation, because people were so self-absorbed it was bringing the country to a social and economical downfall. People were so caught up in their own stuff, they forgot to pay attention to the world around them. Some might say this is representational of just about every generation that came after. I know I've shared my own thoughts about entitled hipsters always looking for their participation ribbon instead of actually having to work to win. That said, I truly believe we are currently in the next me generation.

When we're not posting selfies and tweeting about things we're doing at that moment, we're face down in our phones, looking to see who is doing something without us instead of interacting with the world around us.

Remember our old friend FOMO. We didn't have the fear of missing out in the 1980s. Hell, we didn't know what we were missing out on because it wasn't being delivered directly to us 24/7 like it is for people today. Now everyone is missing out on purpose, and they don't care. Some might be posting something of value to their social networks, but chances are they're trying to find out what they can read to make them feel better about themselves since they've forgotten how to have conversations with real, live humans.

Social decay diatribe aside, if you really want to make an impact with your community, turning them into evangelists for your brand, set aside some time each day to interact with them. Think less about what you are getting out of this interaction, and more about what you can contribute. Reply to comments and mentions, add insight to other people's questions or concerns where you can, and when you see cool stuff from people who follow you, share the love. Give shout outs to people often, and they will love you. Give shout-outs to yourself more, and they may split on you.

One of the key factors behind my own success is how much time I've spent handing out kudos to other people on the various platforms. My friend Sharon relayed an idea to me that she doesn't look at likes and hearts as a representation of her approval, but more like little high-fives, letting people know she appreciates their efforts, no matter how good the content. Imagine if we all took that outlook on things, doling out hearts and thumbs-up because it puts a smile on someone's face, rather than being stingy with them like we're some sort of curator of good taste.

If you think about it, a high-five makes both the giver and the receiver feel good, so why wouldn't we do that more often? Comment, contribute, and share more often, and feel good about helping others feel good.

Sales vs. Sign-ups

When I consult with people and advise them to find more ways to get people on their lists, I often get pushback from the client. They wonder why they shouldn't be looking for more ways to sell to people instead. This seems to be a common concern, because money talks and everything else walks, but the short answer to the question is longevity.

Sales are good, and I want you to sell big. I want you to be tossing hundred-dollar bills on the bed and swimming in them like a rap star. Before we get to that episode of MTV Cribs, though, I want to introduce you to my favorite hip hop star, The Fabulous LTV.

LTV stands for Lifetime Value, and it pertains to how much value a person will provide your business over their lifetime as your customer. This is a common business metric, with a simple equation* for figuring it out, but for our purposes, all we need to know right now is that customer retention is worth more to you than an initial sale.

Yes, you could very well use all the social media techniques I've mentioned to drive people to a link that helps you sell something, and there will be times when you'll want to do that. However, by focusing your energy on getting people onto your list, you effectively increase your chance to sell to them repeatedly.

Hypothetically, let's say you happen to share a post on Facebook that sends people to your products or services. Maybe they'll click through, or maybe they won't. If they don't, the chance they'll see another post by you is slim. Same goes for tweets, pins, or photos on Instagram. If you

---

* Lifetime value = (Average cost of a sale) X (Number of repeat purchases) X (Average length someone is your customer in terms of months or years)

didn't catch them with that post, you may not catch them again.

Now, let's say you did catch their attention, and they did click through. Let's also assume they bought something from you, most likely in a platform or marketplace that doesn't allow you to capture their email address. Yes, you made a sale, but then they are gone. Could they come back at some point? Perhaps, but again, chances are slim. On the other hand, if they had clicked through to an opt-in page and signed up for your list, you may not have sold them anything right away, but you've gained the right to share your goods and services with them repeated. This time you have more control over when they get to see those messages.

Where LTV is concerned, when you gain a sale but no way to maintain communication with that customer, your LTV for that customer is very small. When you capture someone's email address, their lifetime value goes up considerably, because even if they don't buy from you right then, they have the potential to buy from you repeatedly because you are able to actively put opportunities in front of them.

The exception to this rule is when you have an opportunity to capture an email after making a sale, but you must treat those customers with care, making sure they want to receive further offers. If they opt out of getting more offers from you, their LTV plummets again.

The way I like to look at people on my list is as fans first. They joined my list because they liked what I was sharing, and as long as I keep sharing good stuff, they will be fans in good standing. Rather, I remain in good standing with them. If they are good fans, then when I do take some time to promote something to them, a percentage of my readers will buy from me. They buy, not just because they need what I'm selling, but because I provide so much value, they want to support my efforts. Not everyone buys, but even if they don't buy, those people typically remain on my list, allowing more opportunity for me to share and sell in the future.

Also, if I provide big value, keep them as fans in good standing, turn them into customers in good standing, and continue to make them happy, they feel inclined to share what I'm doing with their friends, family and their own followers. If a customer ends up bringing me a new fan, who ends up becoming a customer, the LTV of the first person increases. If they tell two friends, and those two friends tell two friends, and so on, the LTV of the first person ends up somewhere in the millions. OK, maybe just lots of hundreds. Do the math for yourself.

So now ask yourself, do you want to settle for just that one sale, or do you want hundreds? I'm guessing you want to make the Moët and Chandon rain, like any baller would. Get that paper!

Paying for Readers

I would never claim to be an authority on paid advertising, online or otherwise, but I believe this area needs to be mentioned because I know there are many people who use advertising as a way to get people onto their lists. It can be a lucrative idea, if you manage your advertising account with precision.

As far as advertising goes, it's hard to beat Facebook's ability to reach a very specific niche group of people with their promoted post options. To clarify, I'm not talking about using the boost button on posts within your business page. That is paid advertising, but as far as targeting, it's like trying to hit a one-inch target with an intercontinental ballistic missile. Sure, you may hit it, but you'll decimate everything else in a 50-mile radius.

The Facebook ads I'm referring to happen in the Ads Manager section of the site, and through that process, you can narrow down the people by locale, interests, age, sex, and a bunch of other demographics that most other social platforms can't touch. Would you like to gain the attention of some fans of your direct competitor, or a bigger entity that has way more engagement that you? You can do that within Facebook ads. It takes time to manage, but once you find a groove, you can aim your weapon right at the forehead of your future potential readers.

Twitter and Pinterest both have quickly growing and adapting advertising capabilities. Twitter's sponsored tweets are similar to Facebook ads except perhaps a little less exact. You can find some fairly niche areas within Twitter ads, but you may be hitting a lot of people on the fringe of your niche and beyond. Pinterest seems even less targeted, but I've heard from a few people who use them that they are having tremendous success in this area. I will add one benefit to Twitter, and more so Pinterest: Both of these ad platforms are far easier to navigate than Facebook's. The interface of the ad manager in Facebook is arcane and confusing to the newbie. I go there and still fumble my way around, and I've done dozens of ad campaigns.

Twitter and Pinterest recognize that a major benefit for neophytes like myself is to make the system easy to navigate and functionally pretty. Yes, Facebook might be more targeted, but Pinterest helps me get to my result faster and easier. They also have some pretty amazing analytics that are easy to read and identify. From an ease-of-use standpoint, I'd pick Pinterest and Twitter over Facebook all day long. However, if you want to get super targeted, then you'll want to spend your money with Mark Zuckerberg.

All this begs the question, though: Why on earth would you want to spend money to add someone to your list instead of getting them to buy something? At this point, I will redirect you back up to the LTV section. If spending a little bit of money to get people to a list who you know could end up earning you so much more, the question becomes, why wouldn't you? If I can spend one dollar to bring in someone who will eventually give me two dollars, then it is a worthwhile investment. This means that you really do need to run that LTV equation and figure out how much a potential customer is worth to you. If the numbers end up in your favor between advertising cost and revenue, then maybe it's time to get your campaigns in order.

Short Links

When prominent marketers talk about building a list, a word they toss around often is "conversion." Instead of being satisfied with seeing names on the list, they want to know how they got on that list. A conversion is when you put out a call to action and someone follows through. For our purpose, it's when you send someone to your sign-up form and they fill it out. More specifically, when you have multiple sign-up forms, and multiple ways of sending people to those forms, which ones are being acted on the most?

Conversion tracking at its best allows you to see the nuanced behaviors, tastes, and interests of your readers. If you send someone to a single sign-up form, but from three different blog posts about three different subjects, this gives you instant feedback about what your readers are most interested in. The better you get at identifying that information, the better you can cater future information to attract more like-minded readers. There's also the aspect of knowing what motivations people respond to. Do they like positive calls to action that inspire, or do they respond to negative calls to action that give a sense of scarcity, hitting them in a pain point that makes them take action?

The downside to tracking conversions is you can spend your life trying to tweak your content and opt-ins over and over, trying to get the perfect call to action. The problem with this plan is that what hits today may not hit tomorrow, because so many factors are at play. The people who are attracted to your content today may be of a certain ilk, but the ones who find you next month might be interested in slightly different things. No matter how much you tweak your content, reader attention is organic, shifting and changing almost at whim.

So, should you track your conversions? Yes, you should be keeping tabs on what works and what doesn't, but you don't have to overdo it. The single best way I've found to track conversions without it killing your productive time is to use customizable short links. If you've ever used Bit.ly or TinyUrl, you know what I'm talking about. There are other options available, with pluses and minuses to each, but there are two important factors to keep in mind when choosing a short link service.

1. Does the service give you analytics to track on each of your short links?
2. Will the short link generated be considered spam by social outlets?

I use two types of short links for my conversion tracking. The first is Bit.ly, a website that allows you to easily customize your links, and gives solid information tracking stats. The reason I like Bit.ly is that when you enter the URLs from some sites that have their own short link modifiers, Bit.ly will alter your link to fit that website's short link format. It changes amazon.com to amzn.to, which is great for sharing on Twitter, because those few extra characters can mean a lot when you're only working with 140. It's also great for authors like me, because it's Amazon. Am I right?

The other service I use is a Wordpress plugin called Pretty Link, which allows me to create short links based on my own URL. So when tell people to visit FreshRag.com/lac, that actually sends them to my Amazon page for Life After Christmas. Pretty Link also allows me to see my link conversion stats, which is incredibly helpful. Recently, I was wondering where people came from more often to get to the show notes for my podcast, whether through my announcement on the podcast or through social media. With each episode now, I have two sets of links that I create using Pretty Link, and I quickly found that more people are visiting through social media. More importantly, I found that not many people were clicking through to the show notes while they were listening to the show, which was a HUGE eye opener to me.

Before, I was using just one link on all platforms, and although I could see how many people used the link, I had no idea where they were coming from. Now I know that I can emphasize the link less during the recording of the show, and focus more on getting people to it via social media. If I wanted to take this further, I could easily create short links for each social platform, all leading to the same page. This way I would know which social platform was hitting best. If I wanted to get super nuts with it, I could create separate links for different types of posts, or things I posted at different times of day, letting me know when people interact most, and to which content. Honestly, that's more work than I want to spend checking conversions, but some people dig that stuff. Go nuts with it. Just remember that your job is not to check stats, but to get work done and make sales.

Now, why would you use Bit.ly over Pretty Link, or vice versa? I use both sites almost equally, for various reasons, and it typically comes down to functionality. If I had a slew of things I wanted to create short links for, that I didn't need to be branded to my URL, I would use Bit.ly because it's a lot easier to post several links at once. I can bang out a half-dozen short links there in a matter of seconds, but with Pretty Link, it would take me a few minutes to do that many, if I wanted it done with precision. Also, the links from Bit.ly can be even shorter. When you're making a link, they even give you an option to switch to J.mp, which saves you a whole, two extra characters. That's practically a short story in terms of available Twitter space. I'm fortunate that FreshRag.com is a fairly short URL to begin with, but it's not J.mp short.

On the other hand, Bit.ly has its own set of downfalls. Let's say I wanted to use that Amzn.to function, but I also wanted to customize it by making it Amzn.to/authordave. Sorry, can't be done. You can customize a Bit.ly link, but you'll end up with Bit.ly/authordave. Not a big deal, but if you wanted to maintain that Amzn.to aspect, you're stuck with the gibberish extender they put on it.

Also, some social media sites, like Pinterest, will not allow certain short links. I've tried several times to get Bit.ly links into some pins, to no avail. However, if I use Pretty Link, with my own URL, this is rarely a problem. One time I tried to disguise a Bit.ly link inside a FreshRag.com link, just to see if it would work, but Pinterest engineers are smarter than me and saw the link within the link. Granted, I am using Pretty Link Lite, which is the free version of the plugin, but it has enough functionality for most individuals. If you did want to do link cloaking, and needed some other higher-end functionality like alternative base URLs, QR Code generation, and the ability to import and export links, then you can get the Pro version for $40 flat. If you do a lot of affiliate marketing, then you'll want that extra power.

Whatever you do with you short links and conversion tracking, make sure you go in with something of a plan. Figure out what's important to you, and then build upon that. Do you want to track the different social outlets individually? Do you need to go deeper than that? Should you have multiple opt-in pages that you send people to, and then you can track which of those does best? That's a much deeper topic, perhaps one for your next thousand subscribers, but it's something to consider, depending on your need for detailed information.

If you're just getting started with your subscriber list, it may not be a bad idea to have different pages that lead to your sign-up form. You may have a general concept about why people like spending time on your site, but what if you found out those assumptions were off because they were clicking through from content you didn't expect to be popular? This is actually how the current version of Fresh Rag came to be, by simply paying attention to which content was getting the most attention. What started as a site dedicated to showcasing the work of artists who used paper as their medium, quickly turned into a site bent on helping creative entrepreneurs do more with their business. If I wasn't tracking my conversions, I might still be struggling to get paper purveyors to pay attention to me. Instead, I'm here, writing books for people like you, which is where I'm meant to be.

Now go figure out where you're meant to be.

Grow Sales From Your List

One of the things I like to do, with people who look to me for insight, is to anonymously join their list. Yes, I might be on yours and you don't know it. I do this so if they ever ask me questions about their marketing, I know if they're really paying attention to what should be the most important node of their marketing plan. There are three things that most of these people fail to do with their lists:

- Stay consistent with the delivery of their messages
- Provide real value
- Ask for the sale when necessary

What would seem like the most obvious thing you could do with the people on your list is to ask them to buy from you. It's funny to me, though, how often people forget to do that. Maybe it's not forgetfulness, but fear that if they ask their fans for the sale, they will lose those fans forever. But allow me to illuminate you for a moment.

It's important to remember that if you're not making sales, then you don't have a business but a hobby. If you're not OK with asking for the sale, you need to get OK with it because that's how business is done, and if you're not OK with that, then you shouldn't be in business. Sorry, but there is no other way around that idea.

Now, it's not as simple as posting up product and asking them to buy from you. That may work on occasion, but if you do that too often, even your most diehard fans will get tired of it and bail on you. If you go back to those three bullet points above, you'll put yourself in a much better spot to get people to buy in.

Instead of sending messages that just promote a product or service, or on the other side, only talk about things you wanted to write about, what if you combined the two ideas each time you wrote something? Imagine you created a new product and just launched it in your shop. To make people get behind the idea of buying that thing from you, what if you created a story that went along with that product, one that tries to improve the lives of the people reading. Maybe it's a funny story about how you stumbled several times before coming up with the ideal formula for your product, and you've enriched the readers' lives with humor. Maybe it's a tale about how something made you feel when you created it, and that story resonated with some of the people on your list, which made them want your product more. It could be as simple as showing how to use what it is you make in a way that helps them understand the benefits. The more you can make the reader feel part of the story of your products or services, the more likely you are to get them to buy in.

People don't buy what you sell, they buy how you make them feel.

When I polled several of my entrepreneur friends, I asked them how often they pitch product and services to their fanbase. The average was somewhere between 10 and 25%. This means at most, one out of four messages going out was a pitch for a product. What I figure is that every tenth message leaves them with a small exodus of readers, because 90% of the time, those readers are used getting messages that have no pitch. So when the pitches come, it's a bit of a shock.

It's my opinion that you should be doing some sort of ask within each message you send out. It could be asking for a sale, or it could be as simple as asking people to share your message with their friends. This way, people get used to the idea that you ask for things. It goes without saying that before you ask for anything, you must provide value to them with the message. If you've done the value thing, then by all means, ask for something, and do it regularly so they come to embrace that it's how you operate.

If you get down to the base idea of business, it's an exchange of one thing for another. In your case, it's your customer's money, time or attention, in exchange for your product, service, or insight. If you provide them with something of value, whether that's a product, or it's a good story that makes them smile, they are in a deficit within the exchange. In order for them to balance the deficit, they need to supply you with time, attention, or cash money. You tell a story, and they share you with friends. You help them better understand the way things work in your world, and they buy your thing because they feel they know you a little better. It's simple economics, and if you remember to treat it that way, by remembering to sell in your message, than selling overall becomes less daunting.

The Dave Way

When I told the people in my circles that I was writing this book, some of them asked if I was going to talk about my specific strategies to list building, the things I've done that worked and the things that didn't. Not sure why it didn't occur to me at first that you might want to know exactly how I built my list, but, yeah sure, let's talk about this.

Before I get into it, I want you to consider some things before you automatically assume that what I'm doing will work just as well for you. First, my list is not massive. I do not have tens of thousands of fans on my list like some people. My list is substantial considering it's been less than two years since I focused my energy on it, but monstrous it is not.

Second, the people I focus my content toward are people like you. My list-building strategies, for the most part, are based on a business-to-business strategy. Those of you who focus on consumers will want to consider that when you're developing your own strategy.

Third, I trade in information. The things I sell are bits of insight, know-how, and my strategy aligns with that. If you're selling products, your approach may be different. I can write all day long, because the writing is my product, but you may not want or need to write as much as me if you're selling fine art, handcrafted cutlery, or bathroom fixtures.

Finally, I thought about how best to illustrate my strategy to you. Should I share the overall strategy, or chronologically, as I discovered more about my readers? Strategy allows you to see all the working parts moving together, and the timeline allows you to see the victories and challenges as they played out.

I decided chronological was the best way to go because the journey has been quite an adventure, and I think there is more to be learned this way. Of course I will do my best to talk about how all things work together, and how I manage it all. Sometimes I wonder if it manages me, but we'll get to that part too.

The First Gateway

In early 2013, I published a week-long series of blog posts called "Twenty Places to Sell Your Art Prints Online." This started as a single post, but because I tend to write longer than I initially expect (this book was only supposed to be 25,000 words), I ended up breaking it into several posts, each day focusing on a different category of web space. When I published that series, a friend of mine said I should turn it into an ebook. I numbly asked why, and they said it could help me get people on my list.

At this point, my list was a joke. There were maybe fifteen to twenty addresses on it, two were probably mine, and one was my mom. This is how we all start, but then I didn't have a book like this to help me.

I listened to my friend's advice and compiled the list into a downloadable PDF, and gave it away to anyone who signed up for my list. At the time, I wasn't communicating with my list on a regular basis, which we already know is a bad idea. Some of those first fifteen subscribers bounced, probably because they didn't remember who I was or why I was emailing them, even if I was going to send them something for free.

Like many people who are just getting started with their list building, I had only one way for people to sign up for the list, and it wasn't highly visible. People had to click through to a linked page before hitting that sign-up form. This works if you have a nice graphic to draw attention (which I had), but not everyone is going to click through. Compared to where I was before the free PDF, my email list grew to almost eighty names in about a month. I'm doing that in a week now, if not more, but back then it seemed like crazy talk to get that many people on the list. I knew I had tapped into something cool, and did my best to exploit it, sharing the link everywhere I could on social media, to an exhaustive point. I was smart enough to know that all my social links should be pointing to that page, if I wanted to get people directly on the list. This worked for several months, until another friend read the PDF and asked me why I was giving the book away instead of selling it. Lightbulb!

Because I knew this content was hot, I figured if people were talking about how good it was as a free guide, some of them may be willing to buy it if I beefed it up a little. I went back to the manuscript drawing board and turned the PDF into Selling Art Online, and started selling it on Amazon's Kindle platform. Because I was part of Kindle's Select program, I had promised to not provide the book for sale anywhere else, so I pulled it down as a free download, and scrambled to find something to replace it. I also had to radically alter the blog posts so that Amazon didn't think I was trying to give a certain portion away for free. In retrospect, this was probably an extreme move, because Selling Art Online is now in its second edition, and the book is a lot more robust than those original blog posts, and hardly comparable.

Get Up and Dance

After posting the first book on Amazon, I quickly got to work on something to replace it. I had been percolating on an idea for awhile about the more motivational side of being a creative, and put together a short list of things I felt all creative people needed in order to be successful entrepreneurs, I called it Get Up and Dance. At the time, the list sat around twenty items (a running theme with me, I guess), and because I was rushing to get it done, it wasn't nearly as rich in content as the first book. I believed the ideas behind GU&D were important, but not fleshed out enough. I spent more time crafting the cover than I did the book contents, and I think that showed.

I repeated the process of posting the book for free and telling everyone to go get it. Unfortunately, it didn't hit quite as well as the first book. In fact, my sign-ups came to a trickle with GU&D, but my attention at the time was more focused on getting my podcast up and running.

Around this same time, I was introduced to a Wordpress plugin called OptinPress, which allowed me to put sign-up forms in places on my site that I wouldn't have been able to do myself, for lack of coding knowledge. It was also around this time that I had read that article by Derek Halpern about the best places to put your sign-up forms for the most engagement. I quickly went from one or two sign-up forms on my site to several. On any given page, you were probably subjected to as many as six, no matter if you'd seen most of them before. This helped me get awareness for awhile, but I had gotten some complaints from readers that it was too much. Knowing to quit while ahead, I honed my approach, and made it so there were no more than three or four attempts on any given page, one of them being a little sneaky in the navigation.

One tip I got from Halpern was to put a link up in the navigation and call it something like "free updates" or "free tips"-- something that would attract eyeballs to a specific opt-in page. I still use this idea to this day, and it's one of the most popular pages on my site. My conversions on that page are decent, which means people don't feel like they're being duped in any way. This is important to me, because although I am not opposed to using certain sales techniques to gain attention, I never want people to feel scammed, ever.

After several months of using GU&D as my lead magnet, and not seeing the kind of growth I was used to with my first PDF, I did some hard thinking on it. First, I read it to myself again, and being completely self-aware and honest, it wasn't nearly as good as I originally thought. I still believe the tenets were important, almost vital, but I didn't present them convincingly enough.

There was also this itch in the back of my mind that I couldn't quite get at, wondering what problems I was solving with GU&D. Sure, it would help people realize things about their lack of success they might not have considered before, but I didn't help them follow through and turn those ideas into something tangible they could use in their daily life. So I decided to go back to the drawing board and make GU&D more substantial. Because what my rational mind thinks is usually different than what my creative mind considers substantial, I ended up writing a lot more than expected. What was originally ten pages ballooned to well over a hundred. I could have easily pared it back and made it viable even though I'd cut some of the info, but I decided to go the other way with it, which I'll explain in a bit.

I pulled GU&D down as a free opt-in, and instead offered up a piece I had written that I intended as a lengthy blog post called Digital Sharecropping Will Kill Your Business, an ominous tale filled with great content, but an unfortunate name that I believe scared people away. It ended up being my worst lead magnet ever, probably because of the name, but also because nobody asked me to create that information. I won't bore you with the full details, because it really was insignificant to my list growth. In fact, my list size shrunk during this period, which was the opposite effect I wanted, obviously. The lesson, of course, is to make sure the information you're sharing is something your people actually want.

I killed Digital Sharecropping pretty quick, but because I'm a big fan of repurposing, I used the core concepts of that post right here in this book.

Maker's Dozen

After my lack of success with both Get Up and Dance and Digital Sharecropping, I took a long look at why they didn't work: Not only had I not given people something they could implement to increase the growth of their business, but neither solved a specific problem that my readers felt they needed to solve.

I heard a couple of business podcasters once crassly relate business problems to hemorrhoids. The problems are a literal pain in the butt, and when someone has them, the only concern they have is to find a cure, because life is very uncomfortable when you have that problem. People may want what you think they need, but more times than not, they are more interested in what will make their problems go away. Make someone's pain in the butt go away, and they will praise your existence.

Around this same time, there was increasing consternation regarding Etsy and all the things they were doing to increase their own value but not that of the sellers. Since a good portion of my readers are Etsy sellers, I heard all the complaints, and it was becoming a more heated conversation as the days went on. I remember another coffee date with a friend, where we were talking about Etsy alternatives. That's when it hit me what I needed to write next. She helped me come up with names of several alternatives, and I went right home to write The Maker's Dozen—12 Alternatives for Selling Your Handmade Goods Online.

I wanted to keep this one short, but also valuable enough to give people something to chew on. I also tossed in a bonus, making it thirteen alternatives, which comes with a twist.

As it all played out, I crafted a list of alternatives to Etsy, because I know a lot of people were getting fed up with the marketplace. I made it valuable, but not something that took a ton of time to create. I gave it a clever name focused right at the people I wanted to attract, and created an attractive and humorous cover. Then I shared it all over the place, talked about it on my podcast, and linked to it in several places on my site. At this point, Maker's Dozen had become my biggest list generator, and people are still digging it. The only downside to Maker's Dozen is that it's not as evergreen as I would like. Because I'm talking about sites competing in a very tough space, there's a strong possibility that what I mention today will be gone tomorrow. I hope it's not the case, but I keep a watchful eye on those alternatives because I want to make sure the download stays relevant. (This is where I tell you that you should check it out, by signing up for my list.)

With a successful lead magnet doing its job efficiently, you'd expect I would be satisfied to leave well enough alone for awhile, but then I wouldn't be the creative at heart that I am. Soon, I was ready to reintroduce the content I'd originally written for Get Up and Dance, but in a whole new, more kick-ass package.

Creative Badass Challenge

When I got serious about trying to make Get Up and Dance better, I ended up extending the lessons to more than thirty. When it got that involved, I made the decision to turn it into a daily challenge, which has been a popular way to get people to join lists. I have seen creative challenges, meditation challenges, writing challenges, and even list building challenges. It was that last one that got me thinking about this content as a challenge, for a few reasons.

Nathalie Lussier is a specialist in the world of list building, but when I took her List Building Challenge, I didn't think it would become the framework for my own challenge. What I like about Nathalie's challenge is that she gives away her content for free, but she also compiles the content into book so people can do all the lessons, but with the permanence of a book instead of the disposable emails. She gives away tons of value, but also encourages them to buy at the same time. I know her list is in the hundreds of thousands now, and it's changed her life in many ways, so her method obviously works for her.

Following Nathalie's lead, I aimed to do the same with my content, changing the name to the Creative Badass Challenge, which I believe is what you become when you master the lessons I talk about in the challenge. I believe that if you can make it through that challenge, it will change the way you look at your creative life, making you more unstoppable than you were before.

The process of turning this content into a challenge was simple, but definitely not easy. I had to reformat it in a way that allowed people to do daily tasks they could accomplish in a day, but I also wanted to back up each one with content that helped add context. Because I'm a glutton for punishment, I added a short video to each daily challenge, making the content that much more rich, stacking value on top of value.

When the daily challenge was ready to launch, I compiled all the content and made it available for purchase in both ebook and print form. The coordination of all these parts was a struggle, but when it came together, the end result was amazing. I'm not normally one to pat myself on the back, unless it's tongue in cheek, but I am really proud of the challenge.

More than that, I'm prouder of all the folks who have taken the challenge and finished it. It's an honor to have so many people run that gauntlet. It's not easy to finish, and some of it really tests the strength and will of anyone involved, but each day, dozens of people join. My hope is that I'm helping foster a new generation of creative individuals who value their true worth.

My Social Strategy

Much of my personal strategy mimics what I shared in the previous section. It's safe to assume I'm doing all of those things to some degree on each platform. Here, I'll go into specifics but not exhaustive detail about my approach to each. Again, it's important to remember that I treat my business more as a content creator and media company than a producer of products. What works for me may not work for you exactly, but take these ideas and see how you can adapt them to your own strategy.

Instagram

In overall time on social media, I probably spend more of it on Facebook, but that's because I communicate with people there more than anyplace else. As far as commenting, contributing, and sharing with my audience, I love Instagram for the added visual aspect. I get to share some of my own personal tastes as a designer, amateur photographer, and photo stylist. On top of that, I get to see all the wonderful work created by the people who look to me for insight and advice. Sharing our work in this way reminds me of my art school days, where everyone would post their work on the wall and let each other talk about it.

As I mentioned before, instead of choosing a particular image theme, or a style to my photos, I chose to create a pattern with my photos. All my images are grayscale, with gold as my main accent color, which follows my brand. Sometimes I incorporate other colors to the grayscale, but only as a slight divergence. None of this has a direct effect on my list building, but because I make an effort to do something organized and attractive with my feed, it creates a sense of trust and understanding amongst the creative people who visit it. If I give them a reason to trust me, then I open up an opportunity to continue the conversation, hopefully in my email list.

I do send people to my list through Instagram on occasion, but more often than not, I send them to my podcast. This is mimicked on most of my social platforms. This is contrary to the advice I gave earlier, but with a good reason, which I'll get into in a moment.

When I'm posting on Instagram, I use several approaches to draw attention toward links that lead them to my list. Sometimes it's a blatant call to action within the description to get them over to the sign-up form. Because links within the description aren't clickable, I make sure those links are as easy to remember as possible, because visitors will need to remember them enough to type them into a browser themselves.

In the past, I would use the location field to my advantage, by crafting a custom location that said something that gets attention. Unfortunately, Instagram just changed it so custom locations can no longer be used, which is unfortunate. The people at Instagram obviously saw that people were gaming the system a bit (I am guilty) and made a shift to not allow that to happen. Shift happens.

One thing I have tried without success is to write the URL directly onto the photo itself. For me, this has not worked out well. Not only do I not get as many people to visit the link, but I get fewer likes on those images. So, I'm no longer creating those types of images.

IFTTT

Although not a social network itself, I want to mention IFTTT.com because I use it to navigate updates and posts from one social media outlet to another. IFTTT stands for If This Then That, and the concept of the site is simply to allow apps and websites to interact with each other. For instance, if I post something to Instagram, I can set up IFTTT to collect that image and send it to Twitter. You can do something similar within Instagram, but when you use the native abilities, it doesn't send the photo to Twitter, but rather a link to the image. IFTTT allows me to post the actual image as is, along with all the details.

I use IFTTT to send images to Twitter, as well as my Facebook business page, Tumblr, and Pinterest. The reason this is important is to show why I use URLs in in the description of some of my Instagram pictures. That link isn't clickable on Instagram, but when the image gets sent to the other outlets via IFTTT, the description goes with it, as does the now-clickable link.

There are thousands of possible ways to use IFTTT amongst many different apps, and I only have touched the very tip of the top of the iceberg, but these simple actions have helped me manage my content, thus opening up my time. The spare time allows me to do other things, like write books about how to do other things.

Twitter

In 2015, I had two big changes of heart about Twitter. The first that because I wasn't getting a huge amount of interaction there, mostly due to my own inactivity, I wasn't sure how much I wanted to focus my energy. I told myself I was going to do the minimum needed to make it that platform work for me. I started feeding content to Twitter via IFTTT, and I was also using a scheduling app to send out tweets. The functionality was working great, and I was getting a little more interaction, but I wasn't getting a lot of fan growth, which almost solidified my belief in its ineffectiveness.

Even more recently, I had a crisis of conscience, when I realized some of my scheduled content was being regurgitated more often than my actual interaction. Around that same time, I happened to listen to a podcast episode with Gary Vaynerchuk about why he believes scheduled tweets are impersonal and can hurt your brand. Feeling totally conflicted over it, I finally killed off my scheduler. I still push images from Instagram to Twitter, but that only happens a few times a day, and I don't think it's hurting anyone's perception of me, because I share some pretty cool photos. You should see the cute ones of my kid.

My renewed approach to Twitter is simple. I post my links up in my profile, keep my branding consistent, and then when I visit the site or app, I spend my time interacting. I comment, contribute, and share as often as I can. I don't stay on Twitter for too long, only popping in for a couple minutes each time, but I usually hit it a few times a day. My goal there is to build trust in short bursts. I may share links to my stuff now and then, but it's more about interacting than anything else.

Of course, I am using the pinned tweet option to my advantage, keeping it as evergreen as possible, and swapping it out for something new every couple weeks, just to keep things fresh.

Facebook

My approach to my Facebook business page is very hands-off these days. Most of the content gets pushed there, with the occasional organic message, but I largely let IFTTT do its job. I pay attention to who might be commenting, and I reply to comments usually within the day. I have my pinned posts, and my appropriate links, but that is as far as I take it.

Facebook has proven they are not going to go out of their way to share my content unless I pay for ads, so I'm not going out of my way to spend time there, waiting to be served ads from other people.

I do interact with family, friends, and acquaintances on Facebook, and if you friend me up, I will most likely accept your friend request. If you're a creeper who doesn't show much on your profile, with no clue to why you're there, then I likely won't but if you're good people, with an intent to actually interact, or at least consume whatever I share, then I'll accept your friend request. You will likely get served a link or two about my stuff, but I don't hit anyone over the head with it. I talk about the work I do but rarely share links to my stuff there. I definitely expect a certain level of active engagement on that platform, which may be to my detriment, but again, I'm not burning energy worried about what Mark Zuckerberg thinks of my participation level.

I do have my Facebook groups to pay attention to, most notably, the Fresh Rag Army*. I enjoy the groups because I get to interact with cool people, but they also get to interact with each other. I believe these groups help build solidarity amongst our small tribe, and that helps everyone. In there, I do share my work occasionally, but because I made the group as a support system, I don't push too hard. I want people to feel like they have a safe haven to express themselves creatively without being bombarded with pitch attempts. If I know there's something I've done that will help them, I will share it, but only if I know they're going to get value from it, even if that's paid-for value.

Pinterest and Tumblr

Let me be honest; my involvement on these sites is passive. I openly admit that while I have desires to do better on these platforms, I just can't seem to muster the motivation. I recently tried to get more into Pinterest, but it just doesn't give me the same juice that I get from Instagram. My activity there is mostly to maintain some sort of presence, but without spending too much time. Not exactly a strategy, but I do maintain the appropriate branding and links. Instead of fighting my resistance to these sites, I've resigned myself to accepting how I feel about them, which is ambivalent at best. If you love them, then you should rock that all day long. If you're on the fence about them, then take stock of what makes you feel good, or

---

*   Become a creative soldier at www.freshrag.com/army

not so good, and point yourself in the appropriate direction. For me, I'm pointing myself toward mediums that I thrive on, like podcasting.

The Fresh Rag Show

If you aren't familiar with my show, you should check it out. I know I'm biased, but I think what we do on the show is pretty kick-ass. I say "we" because I almost always have a guest on the show, and when they are on, it's more about them and their story than anything else.

The goal of the Fresh Rag Show is to help other creatives do their thing, only better. I want to help listeners feel good about their work, do more of it, and get paid more for it. It just so happens that I feel like I shine in this area. Perhaps it's my love of hearing my own voice, or that I'm pretty good about having interesting conversations that entertain and educate people. If I do those two things when you're listening, then I've done my job.

As far as list building, I try to mention my list at least once an episode. Sometimes I miss it, because I get caught up in other things, but I attempt to spread the love during the episode. The problem being, if you read the section on short links, is that people who are listening to the show rarely take action through the links I provide during the show. Instead, it's the people I bring there via social media that click my links. If they make it to the show notes on my blog, they're going to get served my sign-up form at some point, either by a pop-up or by one of the many links to various content throughout my site. If I get you there, then I've got a good chance of getting you on my list.

Newsletter

This may sound redundant, because why would I want to promote my email list to people who were on my list, but there are times when it's a good idea to talk about my list in the middle of an email blast.

First, if a reader happens to have a friend who might be of the same mind, and needs the kind of content they are getting from me, then I encourage the reader to forward emails to others, and ask the forwarder to share the sign-up page with their friend. Not only does it give me a chance to bring in new people, but because the recommendation comes from someone the new person trusts, they may be more likely to join. Endorsements for the win.

Second, if I happen to have a new list that leads people to secondary content they won't get on the current list, I will send them to that new opt-in. When I made the Creative Badass Challenge, I made sure to send the link to all my current subscribers on the Fresh Rag News, because it would require them to join a new list if they wanted to participate. Anyone who signs up for the challenge ends up back in the Fresh Rag News list, so if they were already a subscriber, the transition is seamless, and I still got to serve them with new, free content. Of course there were also more opportunities to buy from me.

When you're setting up your newsletter, remember that the person reading it may not be the only person reading it. If a subscriber felt compelled enough to share a post with a friend, there's a strong likelihood they know their friend will appreciate more of what I'm sharing. This is precisely why I have some sort of contingency in place that helps get those new eyeballs back to my sign-up form.

It's easy to put a phrase in the bottom footer content of my template to point people in the right direction. Once it's done, it's done, and the process of driving new people to the right place is automatic. The chance of someone sharing that content with another person who will love my content may be small. The percentage of those people that do love it enough to click through to the sign-up form is even smaller, but that doesn't make the effort invalid.

The time it takes to set up the link back to my form is tiny in insignificant compared to the chance to bring even one more person into the fold of my list. One person may not seem worthwhile, but it's possible that one person could end up being my biggest advocate, bringing me lots of sales, and even more attention from people I may have never crossed paths with. Every person is an opportunity to find gold.

Taking That Last Chance

When you get to the end of this book, pay close attention to the pages that come next. Within every book I write, I always include pages with the intent of sharing more of what I do with readers. One page is always dedicated to the other books I have written. Another page points to the podcast, because it is such a large part of what I do. Finally, there's a page letting people know they can find out more about me and my writing just by joining my list.

Those three pages always exist, but I experiment with what order I put them in. Sometimes I put the newsletter information first, and sometimes it's last. One time I experimented by putting it at the very beginning of the book, after the table of contents, because when people view a sample of the book, that's the first page they see. If I'm lucky, they'll read that page and immediately sign up for the list, even if they don't buy my book. That particular book doesn't sell quite as much as some others, but the amount of clicks to that link have been high enough to warrant it's use.

I bring this up, not because I think you should go write books and put your links in the back. Rather, I believe there are places where your fans and customers are seeing you, and you haven't given them a chance to decide if they want to be on your list or not. Instead of putting your regular URL on your business cards, how about a special link to your opt-in page? If you send invoices or receipts to people, is there a way to share the link within the invoice?

From a branding standpoint, some people would argue that if you're not using the base URL only, you're diminishing the impact of the brand. I contend that you not only keep the strength of the brand, but you have a unique opportunity to guide them to a place on your site that could turn them to a customer for life instead of passing interest when they hit your home page and then bounce away.

Take some time to think about all the places you share your URL, and how might you easily adapt that URL to get people onto your opt-in page. Also, look at places where you're communicating with your fans and customers but not sharing your URL. If you can find a way to seamlessly get a link in there, take that opportunity. To give you a boost, here are a few ideas of where to put that link:

- Business cards
- Marketing collateral (postcards, mailers, etc.)
- Email signatures
- Stickers
- Any PDFs, ebooks, or books
- Product instructions
- Guest blog posts
- Product tags
- Receipts and invoices
- ALL social media profiles (Saw that one coming, didn't you?)

The Future

As with many creatives, it can be difficult to judge what my strategy will be any further out than a year. Since adjusting my focus to my writing, finding ways to get people onto my list is a lot more straightforward. Unlike others in my category of entrepreneurialism, I'm not worried about getting people signed up for programs or webinars as much as I am getting them interested in my next writing project. Because writing is what I do, the task of attracting new readers is simply to continue writing high-quality content—content which entertains as well as informs.

One thing I know for certain is that the nature of the Internet is shifting, from static to more dynamic engagement. The simple layouts of websites of the past will no longer be acceptable visually to most people, and will require appropriate functionality to keep the attention of new readers. I also believe the way we gather people onto our lists will change.

Although I don't personally condone data mining of personal information, the truth is, it's happening whether we like it or not. Everything you do on Facebook, Amazon, or any Google properties is being recorded and logged to offer up a future prescription of content that will get delivered to you in one way or another. In the near future, instead of websites pushing whatever content they think you want, the information will be pulled from content farms that gets disseminated to you based on interests you have already shown an interest in.

Your information will come in a centralized hub, and you won't have to stumble through countless websites looking for the content you desire. The stuff you like will be gathered in a central location for you. Of course you'll have the chance to look at things outside of these interests, but that information gets logged as well, and soon you're getting that type of content delivered to you.

When you visit these sites, the content will arrange on the page according to what it already knows about your interests, putting your most commonly read content toward the top in larger segments, with other stories lower, and in smaller sections. As your interests change, the shape and design of the site will dynamically adjust. Traditional website frameworks will be a thing of the past, relying on artificial intelligence to bring you the best content and design. If you had a twin sibling, and that twin spent 99% of the time looking at the same things you did, the information delivered might be displayed vastly differently because of that 1% difference. It's both exciting and frustrating, because while the future seems bright and interesting, this will take the delivery of content out of our hands and put it into the care of code bots.

Taking the concept further, when someone visits one of these dynamic sites, at some point they might be served a sign-up form that tells them they can get more of this specialized content delivered to their inbox, and that content will also be specially chosen. You and your twin might be on the same website, but the sign-up form comes at different stages, from different page sources, and has a separate lead magnet catered to your individual tastes. Once subscribed, you both get delivered content, but catered to what you like, without you ever having to choose your interests.

This possible future is still a few years off, but you will start seeing the potential for it very soon, if it hasn't already happened. Of course, the first companies with this capability will be the ones with big budgets, but it will soon trickle down to the solo content creator. Some sites will still offer up information as they always did, and some of those will thrive, but eventually, the majority of the Internet will be dynamically driven.

In the immediate future, more people will be using automation like IFTTT to help them manage content. Alternatives sites like Zapier.com will do what IFTTT is doing but deeper, with fewer apps, and more focused on helping people do business easier.

In my current email process, when I get people onto one of my lists, the automation sequence is predetermined by me, but soon I will be able to draft several performed emails to go into a sequence, and based on the reader's interests they will get sent a variety of notes from different segmentations of my list.

When it comes to online advertising, Facebook has this functionality called look-alike audiences, which essentially help you created advertising segmentation based on information you already know about your people. Right now, this process is clunky and takes some experience to manage correctly. In the near future, some automation services will be able to gather these look-alike audiences and put them into a chart that is both easy for users to understand, and can be easily deployed within Facebook's advertising interface.

Even more immediate will be the ability to lay out all our content in a simple and 100% customizable way with little to no technical knowledge. Right now, sites like Squarespace give us some control over the flexibility of page design, allowing users to tweak typography, layout, and spatial relationships of elements on the page, but still within certain limitations. As forward thinking as those services are now, they will become arcane quickly. Functionality of site design and, subsequently, opt-in pages, will be so easy to build, you'll fancy yourself a tech genius.

All of that is on the horizon. For now, we manage with our clunky designs, sites visually similar to everyone else's, and that's fine for now. Soon, though, everything will adapt, change, and flow. In fact, the only thing about all this that won't change is your list. Again, no matter what happens, that list remains yours, and no matter what happens, you'll be able to tell your people what is going down. I hope it's always good news.

5

Advanced Practices

If you feel like you're moving quickly beyond the basic and intermediate aspects of list building, then let's move into some more advanced topics. You may have your one thousand subscribers now, but then what? Are you ready to get them buying your stuff? What about if you're managing more than one brand? Do you think you know how to best serve your people, and are you showing them the power of segmentation?

Once you have a handle on the standard operating procedures of your list, and you've become comfortable with the content you're sharing on a consistent basis, you may be ready to take things into those new territories.

In this section, I'll discuss these advanced topics just enough to pique your interest and expose you to the possibilities. You'll have to wait for book two to get the deep dive into these topics, but if your enterprising spirit takes charge, I invite you investigate further. The important thing to know is that there is potential for lists far beyond sending notes to people who gave you an email address.

Segments and Groups

As I mentioned in the terminology section, segments and groups are similar in that they are both are used to organize readers into separate areas to better serve their needs, but operationally they are different. Groups are a way for readers to choose which kind of content they'd like to receive, and segments are a way for you to put them into different categories beyond their knowledge. It's possible for people to be in both segments and groups at the same time, depending on what you need the categories to do for you, but before you start grouping and segmenting your entire world, let's consider some strategy. Too much segmentation could cause confusion, and perhaps give you more work than you want.

Even though customers have some say in what content they receive in groups, ultimately all this information, whether groups or segments, is to help you find better ways to serve. When you're thinking of groups and segments, always keep in mind the core strategy for your list, how you want it to work for your business. You could be looking for more engagement, spreading awareness of your work, pushing for more sales, or some combination of the three. Maintaining a clear indication of your desired end result will help you figure out what segmentation, if any, is right for you.

Groups
The first thing to think about when it comes to groups is that they are best used when you're first starting your list. You can absolutely add groups to your list after you've started, but then you have to go back into your current subscriber list and change the group status of the people already there. If you only have twenty people, then it shouldn't be a problem, but if you have hundreds, you'll have some work ahead of you.

There are lots of ways to use groups to help your readers, but how you break it up will depend on your main objective. How you group people could be based on customer status, gender, age, location, or any other demographic information. Depending on the type of content you're sending, you could group people based on their interests, product preferences, or how frequent they want to be contacted.

More hypotheticals: Let's say someone reading this book has a bath and body product company and they want to best know how to group their people. What might some of their considerations be? Assuming they know the basic core customer demographics, with most being American women between the ages of twenty-five and fifty, living on or near the east and west coasts. That's totally arbitrary information, but if someone knows this much about their customers, then they don't need to group them by these specific details. This customer core is already so niche, then the groups could end up being so specific it wouldn't lend enough information to be useful.

Now, if the customers were more evenly split between male and female, then the business owner may want to group people based on product types, using as many as they felt were necessary to get the point across without being overly analytical. The business doesn't want to create a group out of every product line they have, but perhaps the larger sections of their shop: Makeup, Hair care, Body washes and lotions, Perfumes and colognes, and Men's products.

Another way to look at this business' sending habits would be email frequency. Because their customers may only need to buy products every few months, depending on what they typically purchase, maybe those customers only want to be contacted once a month, while others might want to get something every time the company send an update. They could send out weekly updates to the high-frequency group, highlighting a few new products each time, perhaps with special deals. Then send one main update each month, going out to everyone, including the less frequent readers. If they segment based on product lines, maybe the email blasts are sent each week, but focusing on a different product section, and only going out to the people within that particular group. The more you understand your customers, the better your chances of serving them information that's most helpful to them.

If you understand the demographics of your customers, you can easily group them based on the areas that suit them best. You want to keep your groups simple enough for readers to understand, but rich enough to provide information for your marketing purposes, long term. And remember, even if you have people set up in groups, you may feel you need more segmentation on top of that. The good news is you can always use segments to help you better reach a certain criteria or section of your list.

Segments

The main goals of segmenting are simple: better service, better retention, and better open rates. Yes, you can track data with segments, but what we're most concerned with is creating specialized content that goes direct to a segment of people, thus being more appealing to that segment. The hope is that they become more inclined to opening the notes you send to the their inbox. Your job is to figure out the best way to segment for your specific readership.

Again, you must take into consideration the core strategy of your list, and use that as the target for anything you do with your segments. Since I can't read your mind through this book (yet--I'm still working on that technology), I'll leave it up to you to figure out exactly how these methods might apply to your business.

Just like with groups, you can start by segmenting people with demographics: location, gender, job title, etc. However, you must be collecting this data from your subscribers in order to use it. If someone buys from your shop online and they ask to be added to your list (don't ever add them without permission), you might be able to gather some of that information in your shopping form fields, depending on the e-commerce solution you use. You could also simply ask them for that information when they sign up for your list, but asking for a job title might be a bit weird as far as a general information question. It's definitely not typical of most email subscriptions, but perhaps you have your reasons that wouldn't strike them as unusual.

The power of segmenting might be difficult to imagine at first, but let's play that hypothetical business owner game again. Imagine you have a brick-and-mortar business with a strong local customer base, but also a reasonable number of out-of-town folks coming to buy. You likely don't want to send notices of in-store deals to your entire email list, because many of them won't care, since they don't live in the area. Segmenting your list to include only people who live within a certain radius will not only help get the information to the people who can really use it, but it won't annoy the people who don't live anywhere near you.

Another way to look at localization is to use it for areas you might be traveling to. If you're an author like me, and you're planning a book tour, you could create a segment that includes anyone near a city you'll be visiting, letting them know to expect you soon. Then you can drill down and create and individual segment for each city to remind those readers that your visit is coming soon. The locals will be stoked because you're coming to visit, and the non-locals aren't bothered, because you didn't clutter their inbox with stuff that doesn't pertain to them.

Looking at localization from a different perspective, what if you wanted to know about all the people who might be using Gmail for their email address, and by that, had a Google+ account? Yeah, I know, nobody really uses Google+, but what if you wanted to host a live Hangout On Air with your readers? You could share it with a new segment that included anyone with a Gmail.com email address That way you know those people will have access to your hangout without any problems. OK, so that might be a bit of a stretch, but at least you know you have the power to talk direct to readers based on some of the most seemingly random data, like isolated domain addresses.

Of course, there will be a lot of people who just don't open your emails anymore, if ever. Sometimes people use dummy email addresses strictly for the purposes of getting free stuff from lists but without the bother of having to read the emails. The proper thing for them to do would be to unsubscribe, but instead they sit there, bringing down your open rate. What if you could segment the people who haven't opened your emails in the past six months? You could send them a specific note to thank them for being on your list, but ask if they'd rather not be.

You could take that segment, let them know that if they want to stay, they don't have to do a thing. If they want to unsubscribe, you can give them a link right in the body of the email to do so. If they end up not opening that email either, you can segment all those folks and unceremoniously boot them off your list. No sense hanging onto dead weight that doesn't care about you enough to read any of your messages. You're doing both them and yourself a favor.

I know this sounds counterintuitive, because you worked so hard to get them on the list, but if they aren't opening your emails, then they don't care enough to hear what you're saying. Also, if you happen to be in that space where it's costing you money to have them there, instead of being in the free account level, then you might as well get lose the unwanted and unreceptive names.

Now, there might be reasons why people don't open messages, and you may not be aware of the reason, but you could find out. Let's say someone didn't open your last couple message, but there was some very specific information in the last email that you think they probably should read. You can create a segment strictly for anyone who hadn't read your last note, or last couple, and reach out to them directly. You share with them the special information that you hoped they would read and be interested in, and maybe gain a new sale or two in the process.

On the other side of engagement, there will be some people in your list who are the top of the heap. They read every email, buy your products, and share your stuff with others. These are your cherished evangelists, your VIPs, and you should take special care with them.

Within Mailchimp, they give each person on your list a rating. Everyone starts at a 3-star rating, and depending on their actions, they can either go up or go down. 5-star readers are your VIPs, and you absolutely should have them as a segment so you can reward them for being extra awesome. Maybe it's a super smoking deal on the next big thing you're doing, a freebie that you only give to VIPs, or something as simple as a personalized note letting them know how much you appreciate them.

If you're using a transactional email system like Mandril.com, you can segment repeat customers, or ones who spent over a certain price point, and give them an extra special high-five. You better believe those people will tell their friends if they got something awesome and unexpected from you. If those friends happen to be on your list, they'll wonder how they can get their own high-five.

So you can see, segmentation is powerful, more than groups even, but they can also work together. Depending on your business, I recommend you figure out how to incorporate both, starting with groups to help your readers, and then finding ways to segment later, to help you better identify who the important folks are in a given situation. It'll help you stay relevant to their needs, keep your open rates high, and, hopefully, bring more dollar bills to your pocket.

Segments and Groups vs. Starting New Lists

One of the subjects that seems to come up a lot with the creative folks I run around with is how to manage multiple brands. It's not uncommon for solo entrepreneurs to have two or more different brands or products lines going at once. In fact, when I'm asked for strategy advice, the two most common questions I get are:

1. Should I split my brand in two because of vastly different product lines?
2. Should I combine my brands to make both more manageable and less time-consuming?

You can probably see the cyclical nature of these two dilemmas, and neither one of those questions is easy to answer in a common-knowledge way. The decision should always be based on the wants and needs of the seller involved, and the current status quo will most certainly change over time. You may decide to start a second product line, under a different brand, only to find out later that what you really needed was an entirely new brand, merging the original two, which makes both more streamlined and cohesive—or maybe not. Only you can decide what works best for your business.

I bring this up because as you're making decisions about whether to use segments or groups for your list, there might actually be a need to add an additional list instead. How do you know when to make that choice? Unfortunately, it's impossible to judge without knowing your exact situation. The decision to start an entirely new list, as opposed to segments or groups, comes down to branding, and how you want people to communicate with your brand(s).

If you have one branded line, and you want to add a second line or alternate brand, then segmenting the people on your list according to their interest in each line may not be enough. Even though readers signed up to get updates about your current brand, if the new brand is not something they're interested in, you'll want them to make the subscription decision for themselves. If instead you started a new list just for the new brand, you could announce it to your current list, and give readers a chance to decide which content they want to get updates on, if not both. It sounds like a simple solution, but it has both good and not so good implications.

Let's say your list is 1,500 subscribers strong, and you're still within the parameters of Mailchimp's free account. Then you add a new list for a new brand and invite all your current subscribers to join that new list. Hypothetically, let's assume half of your current list went and signed up for your new list. Now you have a total of 2,250 subscribers across two lists, but you don't really, because many of those are actually duplicates. Duplicates are not a big deal, except now Mailchimp looks at your account and sees that you're over your 2,000 subscriber limit for the free account, and force you to upgrade your account, paying for the extra subscribers. Mailchimp doesn't care that they are the same names on both lists. They just see 2,250 subscribers and want their money. Pay up, sucka!

Those duplicate names inflate your list numbers, and yet you didn't get to add any new customers for your efforts. Sure, those duplicate people might buy from the new brand, but they're still the same people you've been talking to already. The only difference is now you just have to pay for them.

So, if segmenting isn't the right choice in this case, and adding a new list can be problematic, what's the answer? Dividing your parent brand into two groups might be the right away to go. Using the groups, you can give people the choice to join the second group by updating their status within their user settings. It takes some work on their part, but once they're in the group, you can now send separate messages to individual groups, or as a general brand message.

You can also move them to the different groups yourself, through automation, but that means you're paying for automation, and if you're paying, you might as well have separate lists.

On the other hand, if you were thinking of merging two brands into one, and wondering whether to combine lists, that will be your easiest decision thus far. You simply create two groups, one for each brand or product line, and merge one list into another, adding the new list members into the appropriate group from which they came. So simple, it's almost crazy, and super efficient to boot.

No matter what direction you're going with your lists, segments, or groups, the best decision is to always keep your readers in the loop. Don't migrate them without their knowledge, because if you start sending information to them that isn't what they signed up for, they could have you marked as spam, and that could bring a dark cloud over your entire communication efforts. There's no need for unnecessary bad juju.

A/B Split Testing

Within most service providers, there is some functionality to split-test your messages in order to see how certain aspects affect your readership. Split testing, in email newsletter terms, is essentially putting out two different versions of the same message and seeing how people react to each. The differences can be small, like changing a couple words in your subject line, font choice for the body copy, color differences to links, or an entirely different template design of the message. The result being more data on how your readers interact with your information.

You might question how it's possible to find any good data from small changes, at least that could change the course of your email success. The truth is, something as small as using the right noun/verb combination in a headline could radically change how many people see your posts. What if the photo you used in the email repelled some, while another photo got more engagement? You couldn't possibly know that without doing some sort of testing. Most of us go about our business, creating content for our readership and hoping we're doing right by them, but never really knowing if we're doing the best job we possibly can.

What to Test

There really is no limit to what you could test in your emails. If you're lost for ideas, subject lines are a good place to start. Start small by swapping out different modifier words in the same sentence, or test positive motivators versus negative motivators: "This deal is too good to miss" or "Miss this deal and you'll regret it."

Some marketers I know will test the layout of their emails, for instance, switching from a single column, to a two-column layout that has sidebar information. Taking that deeper, you could test the content you're offering in both the main body area and the sidebar. Does an offer work well at the top in the sidebar next to your main body copy, or does it work better at the bottom, with a funny quote at the top? These are all random ideas, but the basic idea is that you test things in small increments to see what works best.

You'll want to work on one area of your messages at a time, testing that portion over the course of more than a few mailings. If you're testing subject lines, make sure to test only subject lines for a few blasts. Once you feel like you've learned a little more about them, then move onto something else. If you're constantly bouncing between test areas. Testing subjects one week, layout the next, and photos the week after that, isn't going to give you any worthwhile data, because you didn't give anything enough time to catch. Think like a scientist, and experiment with one variable at a time until you feel like you've run out of ways to improve in that space.

Contrast to that last statement, when your list is still young, you probably don't want to go too nuts with your testing. First, you've got better things to worry about than figuring out if Times works better than Arial in your emails. Second, the quality of your content is far more important than killing yourself over subject lines. When you list is young, you're still getting used to your readers, what they like, what you like to share. Stressing out over A/B testing might burn you out too early, and you end up losing interest in the platform altogether. Instead, learn to enjoy the process. When you feel like you're hitting a wall with your own growth, then consider doing some testing.

Automation

It's true, robots are in your future, so you might as well embrace them now. By putting the code bots of your email service to work, you can not only help deliver content to your readers in a way that benefits them, but you can also create a flow of content that allows you to do the work early on and let the automation process work its magic over and over for as long as your content stays relevant.

OK, technically, email automation isn't so much robots at work as it is bits of code that allow your service to make judgement calls based on parameters you've set forth. Remember IFTTT and what it stands for? "If this then that" is not an exclusive term to IFTTT, but a standard way of using code to make things happen with many technological things we encounter. When you pressed the buy button on the page where you saw this book, that button was merely a trigger to tell the shop to do something else. The click was the if this, and the then that was the code adding the book to your shopping cart.

Email automation is also an if this then that process, and just like IFTTT, there are many ways to put automation to work for you. For instance, when someone signs up for my email list, they get an immediate welcome message from me, giving them access to whatever lead magnet I promised. From there, they are delivered specialized messages that go out on a regular schedule, but only after they've read the previous message. If at any time they do not get a message, they get halted until they open the last one.

I can set up automation to operate on a timeline according to when someone joined my list, or I can set it up based on a date or deadline. Let's say I knew I had a new book coming out, and I was going to launch it the first week in September, and I wanted to make sure everyone bought on the first day it was available. Sure, I could send a series of emails during the preceding weeks to let people know. Or, I could build an automation sequence way in advance that used my launch date as ground zero and then sent out a succession of emails based on the countdown schedule.

Message one might happen as soon as they joined the list. Message two would hit them two weeks before launch, and message three a week after that, with the final message landing in their inbox on launch day. If anyone jumped into the sequence between certain weeks, they might get the first message, to let them know what was happening, but then skip any messages that were scheduled out longer than the impending deadline. This process takes some forethought and a well organized calendar, but once finished, allows you hands free operation of reaching out to your readers in a strategic way that encourages engagement and sales. Sometimes readers just need a few extra pushes to get them to the purchase decision.

Goals and Sales

If you wanted to get really dirty, you could integrate your email service with your website, and create an automation that gets triggered when a subscriber does something on your site. You give the parameters of certain goals you would like people to achieve, and when they hit those goals, the automation kicks into gear.

Maybe your reader hits on a certain page where you had something for sale, but they didn't buy. You could send them a special note to let them know they have a great opportunity to get a good deal if they want to try again. You could toss in a special discount code for them and link back to the page where they left off.

You could use that same idea, but hit them up as soon as they made a purchase. This time you're thanking them and maybe giving them something special for being a customer and a subscriber. Alternatively, you could send them a note thanking them for the purchase, and maybe recommend another product they might be interested in.

What if you wanted to poll your readers, to gather information about their likes and interests? If you're using Mailchimp, and integrate their survey service, SurveyMonkey, you can send people into a survey during the automation process. Even better, you can turn around and send them into alternate, goal-driven automations based on answers to some of their questions. You could go super nuts and send them into another survey after that, if you felt like dancing with the devil a bit.

RSS-Driven Campaign

As far as automation goes, this is the most basic operation available, and it requires very little management once you set it up. Granted, you need to have a blog--and be updating that blog--in order for this to be worthwhile. RSS campaigns are strictly for anyone who wants to sign up to get notices about blog updates directly into their inbox.

These folks are not like normal email subscribers, and can be ambivalent to whatever else you have going on with your email marketing. The only reason I still have this option available is because ever since Google shut down their Reader app for aggregating blog content, most people don't take the time to check in with the favorite blogs regularly. Since no other app stepped up as a true replacement for Reader, blog aggregation became an afterthought for most. Some readers are still using aggregators, but their numbers were greatly diminished after Reader was retired. Between that, and the proliferation of social aggregation like Pinterest and Reddit, the way we view content on the web has changed dramatically.

In an effort to hold onto a few diehards who like to receive my blog content on a regular basis, I have my own RSS campaign. There might be other ways to use it to help gain attention and sales, but for my purposes, I use it simply to appease a small percentage of folks who prefer getting their content that way.

The only aspect about RSS campaigns that I question is, am I losing out on an opportunity to talk to these people because I didn't send them into a normal email subscription instead? It's hard to say, but my numbers there are so small, it's hardly worth my energy to question it. I don't have to manage now that it's established, and it's not hurting anyone to keep it going. So it stays, for now.

Automation in your email sequences can be quite lucrative if you're using it to your full advantage. Even if all you do is set up a series of emails that get delivered on a schedule for a given amount of time. You're staying actively engaged with your readers. You're also freeing up some of your own time so that you can continue to do the creative work that you're meant to be doing.

Automation is not a cure-all, though. There are clear areas where automation can be a hinderance, for instance, if you're trying to have a personal interaction with your readers, but if you keep in mind that the person on the other end of your automation sequence is still a human being, and their only desire is to get high-quality content from you, then you should be just fine.

Transactional Emails

Have you ever thought of offering a product-of-the-month club? Maybe you're a service provider and you want to share your insight on a certain subject through a paid course delivered via email. There are a multitude of things you could offer as a business to paid subscribers, and there are plenty of services out there that can help deliver those things to your customers.

The problem with standard email service providers, like Mailchimp, Aweber, or iContact, is that they don't have the stand-alone capability to perform these powerful tasks. You can manage the delivery of the subscription-based emails through these programs, but they don't give you a way to have people pay for the subscription to your program, and they can't lock down the information behind a pay wall. You would have to integrate them within a separate membership based service, or at the very least, a pay center, like Paypal or Square. This isn't a big problem, except for the fact that you're bouncing your customer around to different places to handle separate operations, instead of keeping them in one place to manage their flow.

There are services available to help you with all of this, but most of them are incredibly robust platforms, meant for managing not just your email, but almost all aspects of your business communications and product delivery. Services like InfusionSoft, Office Autopilot, and Ontraport can do amazing things and alleviate a lot of work on your end, especially if your business revolves around content management and information marketing. The downside to these services is that they are quite expensive, running anywhere from a couple hundred dollars a month to thousands, depending on the size of your business.

Granted, if you were at the level of needing a service like InfusionSoft or Ontraport, you're doing a lot of business. The cost to use these services then becomes small potatoes compared to the money you're making. Considering you're reading this book, of all email marketing books, I'll assume you're not quite at that level yet. I have hopes you'll achieve that level of success in the future, though.

So, maybe you need a service not quite as robust as the others above but still a lot more powerful than your standard email service provider. To match the demands of some of these other heavyweight providers, but keep it accessible for the little guys, the people at Mailchimp built their own service, called Mandril—a muscled up version of their standard email service. Mandril's main function is to manage what they call transactional emails. What are transactional emails? According to Mandril…

> *"You might simply think of it as anything that isn't bulk. Basically, it is email sent to an individual based on some action. It could be an action they took directly, an action they were the target of or, perhaps even inaction on their part."*

Let's say someone signed up for your email list but then never opened another one of your messages again. Through Mandril, you could send them a single message to remind them that they signed up, ask them if they're getting your messages, and perhaps remind them to white-list your email address.

It could be notes that get sent because someone made a purchase through you, and instead of it being a canned response message via automation, you have their specific data to use in the message. It could be a receipt with a special note, information about their particular purchase, or letting them know when their product will be available based on when they purchased. You could also use it for password resets, welcome messages, marketing emails, and customized newsletters. Mandrill still has holes that some of the other services fill quite well, but the cost-to-benefit ratio tips in Mandrill's favor nicely.

One thing to point out, if you do find yourself looking for a higher-end service like Mandril or the others; none of them are for novices. You'll want to have the phone number of a trusted web developer to help you along with these operations, because they deal in mass amounts of code. Again, more money spent, but if you're in this league, then you're making enough to warrant the cost. Either way, make sure to do your research, because you wouldn't want to get neck deep into something like Mandrill, or worse, InfusionSoft, just to find out that you're in over your head.

6

List Building Dos and Donts

When it comes to email lists, the rules are few, and many can probably be broken, or at least budged a bit. Nobody's going to tell you how to run your list--or if they do, you don't have to listen. Some things you do may end up getting you smacked down by your service provider, because you stepped over the line, but as long as you strive to be a good human in your work, you'll do fine.

That said, I've pulled together a few scenarios that you might want to consider for tried-and-true practices. These are more like guidelines than rules, so take this information and use it as you will.

Stay In Good With Subs

This would seem fairly obvious, but the best thing you can do for your subscribers is to do what you say you're going to do. Provide the type of content you promise, and release that information on the schedule you say you will. Even if it means saying, "I'll only send something to you occasionally, every few weeks," at least you've given them somewhat of an expectation.

Does this mean you can't change your subjects or times? You absolutely can, but consider the degree of change carefully. You don't want to suddenly start sending people notes every week without notice, if they were expecting once or twice a month, especially if those notes are sales oriented. You're better off telling your readers that you're going to step up the degree of posts, and gradually increase the frequency.

The same goes for content. If you're a fashion writer, and you suddenly start talking about vegan living, it might be a huge disconnect for readers. On the other hand, if you said you were going to incorporate more lifestyle content, and made your way to cruelty-free and health conscious living over time, then you're allowing them to transition with you slowly, instead of hitting them over the head with the new content. Either way, you're going to lose some subscribers because of it, because some people think you should always do exactly what you're doing right now. It's unrealistic to think that you will, and when those people leave, wave goodbye with kindness and carry on your merry way.

No, Thank You

Want to know the best way to stay in your subscribers' good graces? Say thank you. Show your gratitude for their attention, and they will stick with you. You don't have to write a post that rambles on about the importance of community. Rather, a simple note that shows your gratitude and maybe gives them a little something in return. That little something can be anything from some heartfelt words to a free giveaway, or maybe a special coupon, but the idea is to make it special. Giving a coupon for an extra 10% off is almost insulting, especially if you give coupons like that on a regular basis. If you want to give thanks, then really give.

Staying In Good With Goog

It almost goes that, if you do the things above, you'll most likely stay in good with Google, and by Google, I mean Gmail. This also applies to MSN, Yahoo, and any other email aggregator. Stay in good with your peeps, and the rest should follow. There are exceptions, though.

Let's say you've been bucking the system and collecting your email addresses strictly through your email application. I know some people still do this, and there's no reason why you can't have a list of people in your application, but if you're routinely sending them messages directly through Gmail, the Goog will probably smack you down. They'll send you to spammer jail, or shut down your account. It's best to be using one of the email service providers that we talk about here instead.

Even if you are using one of the service providers here, you could still get smacked for spam, and it will largely depend on how you're wording your content. If you have a habit of putting the word "free" or "make money" or similar spammy type notes in your subject line, or initial body copy, you're asking for trouble. Not only could your subscribers mark you as spam, but Google has algorithms in place to look for that content, and when they find it, they'll feed it directly to the spam folder without ever hitting the inbox. That's an easy problem to solve—don't be spammy.

Staying In Good With Service Providers

You're going to get the occasional subscriber who bounces off your list because they've decided they don't like what you're doing. They may be bitter about it, and when they unsubscribe, they'll mark one of the negative comment choices that appear as they're trying to leave. It happens to everyone, and you shouldn't worry about the occasional disgruntled reader. However, get a few too many of those red marks on your list and you may catch the attention of your service provider. If it happens often, you will be blacklisted, unable to continue sending notes.

There's a good chance you have nothing to worry about, unless your purpose is to send out tons of spam to people who never really opted into your list. If you do that, well then, I can't help you. You're on your own, because that's not what this book is about.

Now, if you're playing nice with your subscribers, and staying friends with Gmail, then you shouldn't ever feel the pressure. If for some unknown reason you start getting some red flags, the best advice is to contact your service provider right away to find out what you might have done wrong. They want to keep you in good standing, so they will try to help you figure out the problem. Since they see millions upon millions of emails in their system, they certainly are more aware of potential problems.

Republished Blog Content

This isn't a hard fast rule, but seems to be a trend among some small businesses. They write a nice post on their blog, and turn around to post it to their newsletter. Doing this occasionally is perfectly acceptable, especially if your're trying to get subscribers to interact with a specific post. What I like to do in those situations is only share a small portion of the post in the email, a teaser of content, and then send them to the blog post with a link saying something like, "If you want to read what happened next, check it out on the blog."

That strategy works quite well when I do it, but I used it sparingly. One of the things I cannot stand is when I sign up for an email newsletter only to find out it's nothing more than the blog repurposed. If you want to provide that for someone, then use the RSS campaign function, and let people who sign up know that they are only going to get the content from the blog. Otherwise, what's the point of being on your list if all I'm getting are the same things anyone has access to on your site? As a reader, I want to feel special, and regurgitated blog content is not special.

One option would be to post a recap once a week, or every few weeks, sharing snippets of all the posts you've written in that time. That way the reader can pick and choose what they want to read, and it's not the exact same thing they can get on the blog.

Customers Are Not Subscribers

Just because someone bought something from you, that does not mean you have permission to add them to your email list. The only obligation you have to them is to contact them about their purchase if necessary. If you add them to your list without permission, they may report you as spam, and then you have the problems I spoke about above.

This also applies if you go to an event and collect a bunch of business cards from people. Jennifer Pierce of Hydrangea Hippo had this to share on the topic: "I hate when I come home from a conference and I gotta unsubscribe from a bunch of stuff I never signed up for. I feel like that is the worst way to tell me you want to do business with me. [My process is to] add all the business cards to a list, send them one email, and give them the option to subscribe."

If you want to turn your buyers into subscribers, send them one note post-purchase and give them a link to your opt-in page. Make it compelling, and sell them on the idea of joining the list, but if they don't respond, leave it be. If you're respectful of their space and email privacy, maybe they'll come back and buy from you in the future, or better, join the list eventually.

Do NOT Buy Lists!

I can't stress this one enough. Yes, you can do it, but I believe it to be bad business. You may be able to find a list for sale that says it's filled with people who are your ideal customer, but because they never signed up for your exclusive content, you're asking to get lots of people flagging you for spam. No matter how meaningful your intentions, using a purchased list of email addresses from people who don't know you is the fastest way to get yourself blackballed.

W.I.I.F.M.?

That stands for "What's in it for me?" and comes courtesy of my good friend and fellow author, Berni Xiong. She says, "It's not about you. People often think they have to sound smarter or be an expert when they share their goods with their subscribers. But in all reality, the reader is only thinking about one thing...'What's in it for me?' They're giving you their time and attention because they believe you might tell them something different that they haven't already heard anywhere else. They don't care about how awesome you say you are unless it's to teach them how they, too, can be awesome. Make it about your reader. Show them how they can be the hero in their own story. Most importantly, be you. No one has time for another imitation of the guru making six figures a month. People trust real people. Keep it real."

Stalk Others

Sometimes we get stuck for ideas. We think we're moving along, generating quality content, and then we find out that we've become boring. We may want to change things up, but since we've moved into Boringville, we've forgotten how to innovate. Hopefully, as a marketer, you are also subscribed to a few lists, and within those lists there are some that you really admire. Instead of worrying yourself over what to post to keep from being boring, just pay attention to what others are doing, and repurpose the idea for yourself.

A little clarification for anyone who scoffs at the idea of stealing others' content. You should absolutely not plagiarize anyone's work, but if someone has an interesting way of presenting their work, and you could alter it to fit your own content, then by all means, do it. Chances are that person got their idea from someone else, anyway. There are very few truly original ideas in this space anymore, but that doesn't mean you can't make yours unique.

One last caution: Tread lightly if the person you're admiring happens to exist in the same niche as you. If you do the same sort of work as them, it's probably not a good idea to copy their format, even if you are using original content in their template. Someone who likes both of you is going see your message and maybe run off and share your appropriation with the originator. Not that you'll get into any real trouble, but beware the backlash nonetheless. Go find someone outside your area of expertise to borrow from instead.

Also straight up copying is boring, and you don't want to bore your readers with something they might have seen before. Borrow with grace, and make what you borrow into your own [props to my editor for reminding me to add this last bit].

Distraction-Free Pages

This isn't always easy, but if you're using a third-party app like Lead Pages or Optimize Press, you can create landing pages that serve one purpose: getting people to sign up. The common understanding is that if you have too many other things on the page, people get distracted by shiny object syndrome, and they may find a reason to leave your page before signing up.

Full disclosure, I no longer use Lead Pages myself. I did for awhile, and I was reasonably happy with their service, but as a designer fixated on maintaining my brand, I was disappointed that I couldn't get the page templates to line up with my branding exactly as I wanted. The templates took on a very internet marketing* feel, and that didn't fit with my aesthetic.

Instead of using a third-party app, I have a website service that allows me to create my own landing pages. They sometimes aren't completely distraction-free, but they're close to it, and it works for my purposes. You should do whatever feels most authentic to you and your own brand.

Cross-Reference to Mobile

As each day passes, a larger percentage of people are viewing your content on mobile first. When crafting your messages, make sure you're checking to see how those messages get relayed on a mobile device. When I was with Aweber, they didn't have this function, and it was frustrating because sometimes my messages looked really bad on mobile. It was one of the reasons I left the service and jumped over the Mailchimp. I don't know if Aweber has remedied this problem, but Mailchimp gives you the ability to see each message, in both mobile and browser mode, as you're crafting it. This alleviates a lot of headache, and will help you retain subscribers because you didn't make them work hard to read your stuff.

Ask For Shares

There's an interesting phenomenon I've seen with some of the business owners I work with. A lot of small businesses feel like it's an intrusion to ask their readers to do something for them, like buy something or share content with their friends. The thing is, your readers joined your list because they like what you're offering. If they didn't like you, they probably wouldn't have opted in. At the very least, they won't stick around.

There's nothing wrong with putting out the call to your readers once in a while to ask them to share your stuff. The frequency of which you ask is up to you, but don't be afraid to put it out there. If you're bringing them big value on a regular basis, it's hard to imagine they would have a problem sharing it.

Granted, only a small percentage will follow through with the call to action. If you only get a few people who actively share your content, don't stress over the quantity but be appreciative of the ones who did. Those are the people you should be sending thank-you notes, by the way.

7

The Definition of Value

Throughout this book, I've brought up value numerous times. Before we wrap it up, I wanted to clarify my definition of value, because it may not mean what you think it means. In truth, it could mean what you think it means, but also mean something else.

Some might define valuable content as lengthy posts that share wisdom about a certain subject, process, or situation. Although those may be true cases for value perception, they are not the only value that one can bring with their lists.

The value you bring to your readers should be defined by two simple factors: you and them. The value comes at the crossroads of what you believe is the right type of content to share, and what information the reader is hoping to get from you.

For me, my value comes in the form of stories that have lessons. This is what I've done all my business life, and it's what I've done with you throughout this book. Everything people get from me is based on experiential knowledge of the world around me, and I like to share it through storytelling. I'm a writer, and writers write. You may not be the same kind of writer, and that's OK.

Whether you tell stories, or create how-to videos, share pictures of your travels, or simply send out quick notes about the cool, new thing that went live in your shop, the value is not defined by anybody else's perception except yours and the reader's. If all you want to do is let people know when new products drop, and all your customer wants to do is buy--with the hopes of getting a coupon code—give them a code and you've created value. Writers write, makers make, entrepreneurs entrepreneur, and nihilists don't care. Still, though, if the nihilist has a list of people who love them for their nihilism—BOOM! Value.

Don't let anyone tell you what's valuable and what's not. If you don't want to share a lead magnet, because you think they're dumb, then don't. That is perfectly OK. Someday your readers may let you know they want that freebie from you, but for now, you keep rocking things how you see fit.

#DoTheWork

Now you have no more excuses. Truthfully, you didn't have any before, but now you really don't. It's time to drop the stick into gear and get moving on making things happen. If you haven't started your list yet, the best thing you can do right at this moment is to take action and start your list.

Do not hesitate, do not find reasons to hold off, and do not let anyone convince you otherwise. The sooner you get this going, the quicker you can start filling your list with people who want nothing more than to know more about you and the work you do.

If you've already started, and you're looking to grow it faster, ask yourself what things you have learned in this book that you've been avoiding or didn't know were possible. If you haven't done this already, write any and all ideas down, and when you're done, prioritize them. If you need help with priority, the first thing you should do is send them an email. If you've been noticeably absent, maybe a note to say thanks for being awesome. Do not apologize, though. Nothing irritates readers more than when you make excuses for not doing what you said you would. They'll bounce from your list faster than you can say, "The best thing you'll read all day." Instead, acknowledge that you haven't written in a while, and let them know that you have a renewed vigor to give them exactly why they signed up for. Maybe you'd like to tell them a certain author with a kick-ass book on email marketing made you realize the error of your ways. I'd be OK with that.

The point is to make you feel awesome about being there, and then ask them to share it with others, because you want to make sure more people get the awesome for themselves.

Next, write some quality content to share with new people when they sign up. If you're just about to go all in on your newsletter, might as well have some potential posts at the ready, even if you're holding off on sending until later. In the free Mailchimp account, you can't schedule posts or set up automation, but you can still have draft messages waiting for you to hit the send button. Stack a few up, and maybe craft a teaser of what's to come, to kick things off.

After that, work on better ways getting your sign-up forms in front of people. Can you put it in the header? Do you need a pop-up? Maybe you can experiment with versions in your sidebar. Make it fun, play around, and experiment.

Once you have all those basic ingredients in check, now it's time to start sharing it on social media. Let people know you've got a list, and if they want to know more about what you're up to, they should join. Add your sign-up links to your social profiles, and wait for the hordes to storm the gate of your opt-in page.

Remember to maintain the value proposition, especially if you've been absent from your newsletter for awhile. The first few blasts you send out should be all about the reader. Technically, every message you send should be all about the reader, but these first few should be singularly focused toward them.

At this early stage, you have two objectives. First, make your current readers as happy as you possibly can. Second, find ways to attract more people. Once you feel like you have some momentum, and people are telling you how much they enjoy your emails (it won't be a lot, but there will be a small percentage), then you can start with the pitches. Use those pitches sparingly, but dropping the occasional hint that you have things for sale, along with creating killer content, will encourage fans to support you for all the hard work you've done for them.

You will spend a lot of time and energy on this list, and it may seem like too much work for something you might not be 100% convinced on. I promise, though, if you share good stuff with your email readers, they will reward you more than any other outlet. If you spent a little less time on your blog, your shop, and your social media accounts, and invested that time into our list, you'd see results. Once you see the results, you'll know that your time is best spent talking to the people who have declared they want to hear more from you.

Normally in my books, this is where I break out the pom-poms and cheer you on, telling you that I believe in you, giving you virtual shoulder rubs and a smack on the butt as I send you back out onto the field. I absolutely do believe in you, because despite what you might think about this email list stuff, it's simple. It's not always easy, because of all the work involved, but it's definitely simple.

I believe in you, but I know you got this, so no more cheerleading. Now it's time to do the work, make stuff happen, and start bringing in the people who may end up being your best customers ever. I'd wish you luck, but I know you don't need it. Do what's necessary and important, and your future is certain.

Now, get to work.

Resources

Email Service Providers

There are many, many options available for email service providers, and this could have been an an extremely tiresome list. To avoid too much confusion with an embarrassment of choices, I've gathered some of the most popular and respected services, delivered in no particular priority. You already know which I recommend, but there could be one below that better suits your needs and tastes.

Lite
- Feedblitz.com
- TinyLetter.com

Business
- Aweber.com
- BenchmarkEmail.com
- Campaigner.com
- Campaignmonitor.com
- CheetahMail.com
- Constantcontact.com
- ConvertKit.com
- Friendlybriefs.com
- GetResponse.com
- Graphicmail.com
- Icontact.com
- Letterpop.com
- MadMimi.com
- Mailbuild.com
- Mailchimp.com
- Myemma.com
- Respread.com
- Shoutlet.com
- Whatcounts.com
- Ymlp.com
- Zookoda.com

Advanced/Transactional
- Infusionsoft.com
- Mandril.com
- OfficeAutopilot.com
- Ontraport.com

Third-Party Apps

Hello Bar

You've probably seen these around on random websites, but they are steadily losing their appeal because so many new Wordpress templates are implementing easier ways to get elements like sign-up forms into the header of a site.

The Hello Bar is a narrow bar that runs across the length of your site, can be matched to our branding, and allows you to either get people onto your list, or send them to a special page either on of offsite. With the proliferation of the more dynamic themes, and other plugins that do the job more efficiently, Hello Bar will probably cease to exist in the coming years, but there's reason why you can't try it now.

Hello Bar comes with either a free and a paid version. The free version allows limited control, and you're forced to keep the Hello Bar branding on the bar. The paid version gives a lot more control and removes the branding. I would personally choose the free version until you were ready to make a serious upgrade, with either your site's template or a more qualified plugin, like our next entry.

Pop-Up Ally Pro

There are a lot of pop-up programs and plugins available on the market, but none are better at handling pop-up tasks quite like Pop-Up Ally. From a design standpoint, it's incredibly flexible, giving you a ton of control over dimensions, colors, font choices, and content. It also has a strong control system in place that lets you to create a hierarchy of pop-ups, allowing some to show before others, depending on where your visitors are on your site. You can also choose the frequency of pop-ups, making sure people who come to your site often don't get repeatedly hit with them each time they visit.

The plugin also does more than pop-ups. You can create standard forms to appear within certain parts of your site, like the header, footer, and sidebar. You can even create a full-width bar, similar to Hello Bar, but with a lot more control.

Pop-Up Ally is a Wordpress plugin only, and comes with a high price tag for a plugin, but worth every penny. If you manage multiple brands, and multiple sites, you should opt for the developer license, which costs a lot more, but gives you the ability to use it across any site you see fit, even if it's not your own. This is a great purchase for web designers, developers, or people who just have a lot of websites.

Crazy Egg

If you ever wanted to know how people interact with your website or, more specifically, how people are interacting with your sign-up forms and opt-in pages, you might take a look at heat mapping software. Anyone has the ability to track clicks on your site, seeing where people are spending the most time. What about the people who meander across your pages, but don't click that often. What if you could tell how people read your content as it hit them, and where they move their mouse around the page? With Crazy Egg, and apps like it, you can implement a heat map that shows the most active parts of your page. If you can imagine a weather map that shows the color coded hot and cold areas of the map, then you know what a Crazy Egg heat map looks like.

When someone spends a lot of time on a single page, or in a certain part of a site, that information gets logged and shows up as a heat zone. Also, when visitors hang out, and they move their cursor around the page, because often a person's cursor will follow their eyes, the areas that get lingered on the most show up hotter. So, if you were curious to know where the best places would be to put your sign-up forms on a page, a heat map service like Crazy Egg could help.

Lead Pages

This is a sales and opt-in page service that allows you to add somewhat customized page templates. Through Lead Pages, you can integrate sign-up forms and content-driven sales pages that have a proven track record of getting more conversions. The templates are limited, but each one has added customization, to a point. Not all elements on the page are customizable, but enough to make them interesting and still match your website's brand.

Short Stack

Short Stack's focus in on helping you create contests and sweepstakes within your social media while capturing data like email addresses. It integrates mostly with Facebook, and can help you add more people to your list by giving them ways to interact with contest-based content.

Truthfully, I know very little about Short Stack, and I know they have been stymied by Facebook in the past because the app was gaming the system Facebook already had in place. Short Stack worked through that stage and are operating within Facebook's parameters, but that could change quickly. Facebook continues to spend more effort integrating new technology, focusing more on keeping people on the site instead of sending them offsite, which is what Short Stack does. I can't imagine Short

Stack being a long-term play, but you can use their services now to garner some attention.

IFTTT

I've already talked extensively about IFTTT throughout the book, so I won't go too deep. This automation sequence service allows sites or applications to communicate and digest information in a way to automate certain processes. You can use it to send information from one social media platform to another, add your images and content to your drop box, or even manage home automation with smart accessories. The only thing you can't do is anything with Mailchimp, but there's an answer to that situation.

Zapier

This site is similar to IFTTT but has deeper functionality than its competitor in some specific areas. For instance, with Mailchimp, I am not able to easily move people between lists unless I want to migrate them into each other completely. Sometimes that's OK, but other times I want some of those people to be on both lists. Zapier allows me to set up functionality that can move people from one list onto another based on their reading habits, or when they hit a certain section of my Mailchimp automation sequence.

At the time of this writing, I have very limited experience with Zapier, but as an alternative to IFTTT, and with the added functionality of working with Mailchimp, I'm going to be digging deeper into this app. Stay tuned to my email newsletter to find out more. You can sign up at www.freshrag.com/news/.

Other Important Links

Writing Good Subject Lines

"Best Practices for Email Subject Lines"
bit.ly/subjectbestpractices

"How to Write Magnetic Headlines"
bit.ly/magnethead

"10 Sure-Fire Headline Formulas That Work"
bit.ly/surefireheadlines

"18 of the Best Subject Lines You've Ever Read"
bit.ly/18subjectlines

Ideas For Your Email Blasts

"33 Email Newsletter Topics You Can Use Right Now"
bit.ly/33EmailTopics

"15 Email Newsletter Examples We Love..."
bit.ly/15newsletters

Online Advertising / Paid Traffic

The Art of Paid Traffic Podcast
rickmulready.com/aopt-podcast-all/

"Succeed With Pinterest Promoted Pins"
bit.ly/pinterestprompins

"The Definitive Guide to Twitter Cards"
bit.ly/twittercardsguide

Screen Capture Software

Camtasia (Mac and Windows)
www.techsmith.com/camtasia.html

Screen Flow (Mac only)
www.telestream.net/screenflow/overview.htm

Webinar Software

Google Hangout
google.com/hangouts

GoTo Webinar
gotomeeting.com/webinar/

Adobe Connect
adobe.com/products/adobeconnect.html

Useful Wordpress Plugins

Pretty LInk Pro - Short Link Creator
prettylinkpro.com

Optimize Press - Sign-Up Form Templates
optimizepress.com

Miscellaneous

Lifetime Value Calculator
bit.ly/ltvcalc

Join The Army

Now that you're done with this guide, if you still feel lost or confused by any of it, I invite you to come join my free Facebook group for creative business owners, the Fresh Rag Army.

Join, pose your questions, and not only will you get direct access to me, but have a legion of people who have been down this road, and are willing to help.

You can join at www.freshrag.com/army. If you can't get your question answered there, either by me, or others in the group, then maybe the question can't be answered. I highly recommend you head over and join.

www.facebook.com/groups/freshragarmy/

About the Author

Dave Conrey is an artist, author, and podcaster. When not spending time playing dinosaurs and robots with his son, he is working on a number of creative projects, ranting on his podcast (The Fresh Rag Show), or writing his next book.

Before launching his own brand, he worked for two decades as a marketing professional and art director, and he uses this experience to inform, engage, and advise creative entrepreneurs on how to take their work from a hobby to a viable, thriving business. Visit daveconrey.com to find out more.

Also by Dave Conrey

Selling Art Online
The Creative Guide to Turning Your Artistic Work into Cash

Life After Christmas
Branding, Design, and Marketing Strategies for Small Businesses

Creative Badass Challenge
One Month to Change the Way You Live and Work

You can find all of Dave's books on Amazon.
www.bit.ly/authordave

Three More Things

Get On the List

First, if you haven't yet had an opportunity to join my list, the best thing you can do to keep tabs on what I'm doing, or what techniques I'm using to improve my business, then head on over to www.daveconrey.com and sign up today.

Ratings and Reviews, Please

As an independent author and publisher, the way I get the word out to more people like you is through ratings and reviews. Now that you're done with this book, I would surely appreciate you taking some time to review it at www.bit.ly/goldlistbook

You are Awesome

Now go make some more awesome things happen.